COLLEAGUES

COLLEAGUES

JOHN RETALLACK AND ANNE C. COON

RIT CARY GRAPHIC ARTS PRESS
ROCHESTER, NY

Published and distributed by
RIT Cary Graphic Arts Press
90 Lomb Memorial Drive
Rochester, New York 14623
http://carypress.rit.edu

Designed by Marnie Soom

ISBN 978-1-933360-52-2

Library of Congress Cataloging-in-Publication Data

Coon, Anne Christine.
    Colleagues / poetry by Anne C. Coon ; photographs by John W. Retallack.
        p.   cm.
    ISBN 978-1-933360-52-2 (alk. paper)
    1. Photography, Artistic. I. Retallack, John W., 1941– II. Title.
    PS3553.O5758C65 2011
    811'.6—dc23
                                                        2011015021

CONTENTS

INTRODUCTION
Anne C. Coon, Ph.D.
Professor Emeritus, College of Liberal Arts, RIT

In 2008, John Retallack and I began putting our work together—his photographs and my words. Since then, we have collaborated on several pieces; in most cases, I have studied images from John's portfolio and written a poem or series of poems in response. We have also experimented with the opposite process, starting with a poem of mine, for which John created a photograph.

This book has a different creative genesis from our other collaborations. The collection of photographs represents several years of John's work making portraits of colleagues at Rochester Institute of Technology. Although I was one of those who sat for a portrait, I also agreed to create a text to accompany the photographs. As I was writing "Enter the Eyes," a reflection on sitting for and looking at a photographic portrait, I became increasingly curious about John's thoughts about the images.

Thus, I posed to John some questions about the work he prefers to call "photographing people."

What's most important to you when you make a portrait?
Most of the time I don't have a conscious, preconceived idea. It comes together when the person is in the studio and a relationship develops. Sometimes there's a definite idea or approach I want to take. For example, shooting with the light underneath. There's a rule against that, but I wanted to try it. I did about six successful pictures with that technique. Setting up the studio in advance is also important. I photograph myself to see if the lighting is right, and so have created a series of self-portraits.

How do you establish the relationship with a subject?
Talking, being with the person. Once in a while it doesn't come together, and then in a single frame it might happen. Sometimes the art of photographing people is pushing the button at the right time or *creating* the right time to push the button. That's why the set has to be ready when the person walks in.

Does knowing your subjects matter when you're taking their pictures?
Once they're in the studio, it doesn't matter because it's all about the relationship that develops.

Do people ever try to give you advice, such as, "this is my best side"?
Sure. I usually do try people's suggestions. Maybe it is their best side, but going along also makes them willing co-conspirators, and then we're free to move on and try other things.

How do you describe the portraits you make within the tradition of photographic portraiture?
I'll answer by describing what I think is a successful photograph. When you look at one of my portraits, the person seems to be himself or herself. Someone who knows the person would recognize that expression or side of their personality. That happens when light comes together with the person's expression and attitude. I'd say that's the unique quality of my photographs: light coming together with the person.

Did you take pictures when you were young?
When I was a kid I had some encouragement. I remember a little Kodak Brownie camera I used to take pictures of my schoolmates in 4th grade.

How did you get started doing portraits?
My interest in portraiture came well after my development as a photographer. After I was in the service, I was living in a small town in Michigan. I missed the friends I had made in the Army, and I started taking pictures. When I began working as a photographer in New York City, the normal path was to be an assistant, so I worked with three better-known advertising photographers, *photographers of people*, for about two and a half years, in the early 1970s.

What do you mean when you put the emphasis on *photographers of people*?
At RIT, I taught "Photography of People," not "Portrait Photography," because the word "portrait" has unnecessary connotations. People think of a stylized head and shoulders photo with a conventional studio approach. This is what people expect and feel comfortable with because it is an established genre. For my course, in addition to the usual assignments, I asked students to submit at least a half-dozen photographs of a person's feet. They didn't have to print or critique the photographs but to hand in a proof sheet to show they did it. There were a couple of reasons why I gave this assignment: First, feet aren't pretty, so the photographer had to adopt some stylistic approach in the photograph. Second, the challenge of it. Photographers need to develop the ability to rise to a challenge. Students need to learn to *enjoy* that.

What makes this project unique from your other work?
The photographs are all black and white, and all digital. Because they are digital, they start out in color, and I can take different parts of the spectrum. In shooting black and white, I pay more attention to light than to colors. Colors are not relevant unless they have an impact on how they will convert to black and white. In the old days of black and white—the heydays of the 30s and 40s—photographers used yellow filters to photograph women and green filters to photograph men, to give an appearance that was softer or more ruddy. This applies to how I convert the color digitized image to black and white. Knowledge of past photography gives me more control. The conversion of color to black and white is variable, and I always look at how it can be manipulated to improve the picture, or more specifically, a person's *perception* of the picture.

What would you want to do if you weren't a photographer?
If I couldn't be a photographer, I'd be a writer.

Do you see your photographs differently when there are words with them?
Words can add meaning or point a picture in an unexpected direction, or restrict it. In advertising, when the words and picture say the same thing, the communication is mundane. It's a delicate balance. Words and pictures together, when it works right, can be a symbiotic relationship. Something new is created from combining the two.

What follows, then, is *Colleagues* by John Retallack, combined with "Enter the Eyes" by Anne C. Coon.

COLLEAGUES

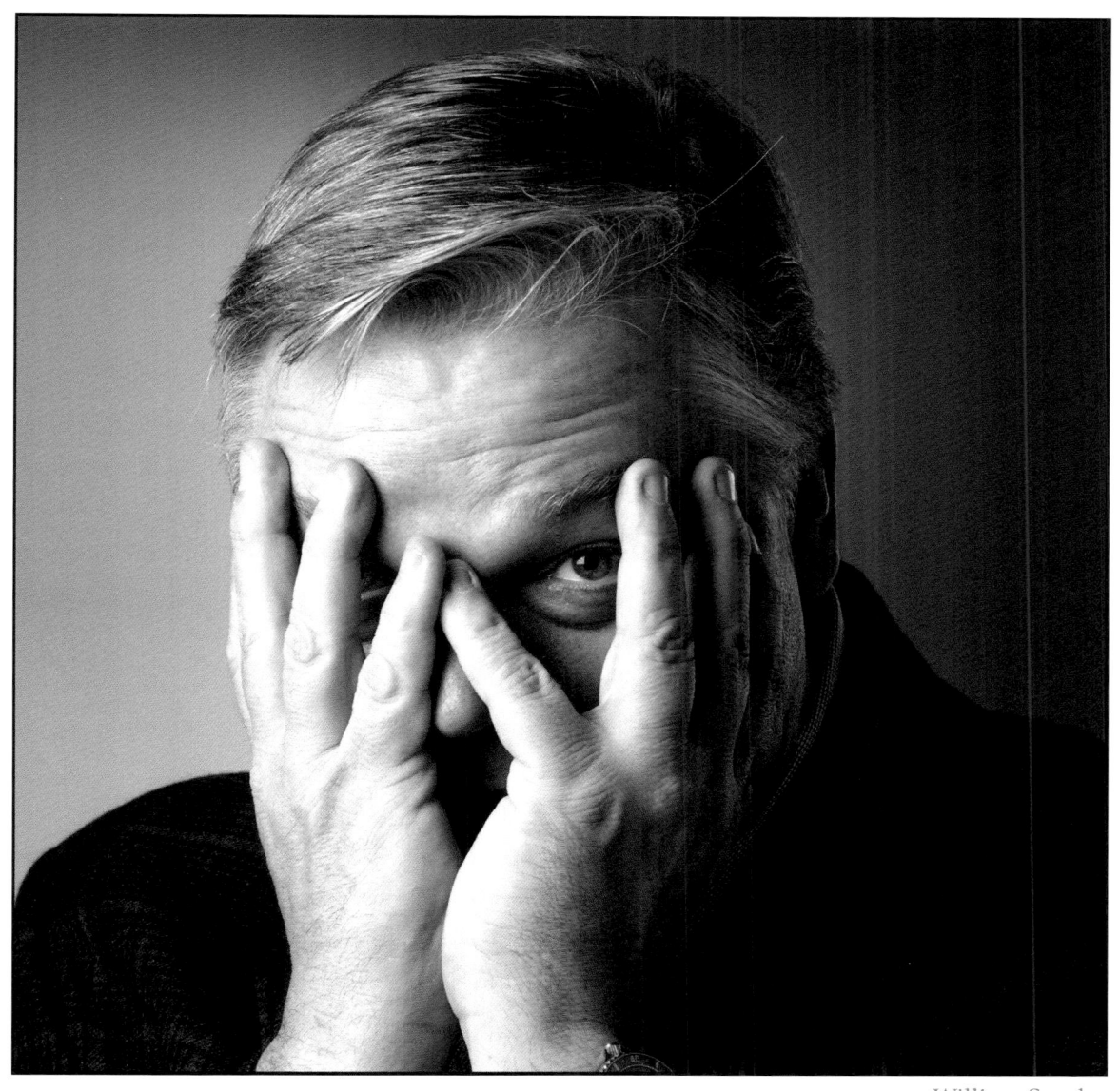

William Snyder

Confront the gaze

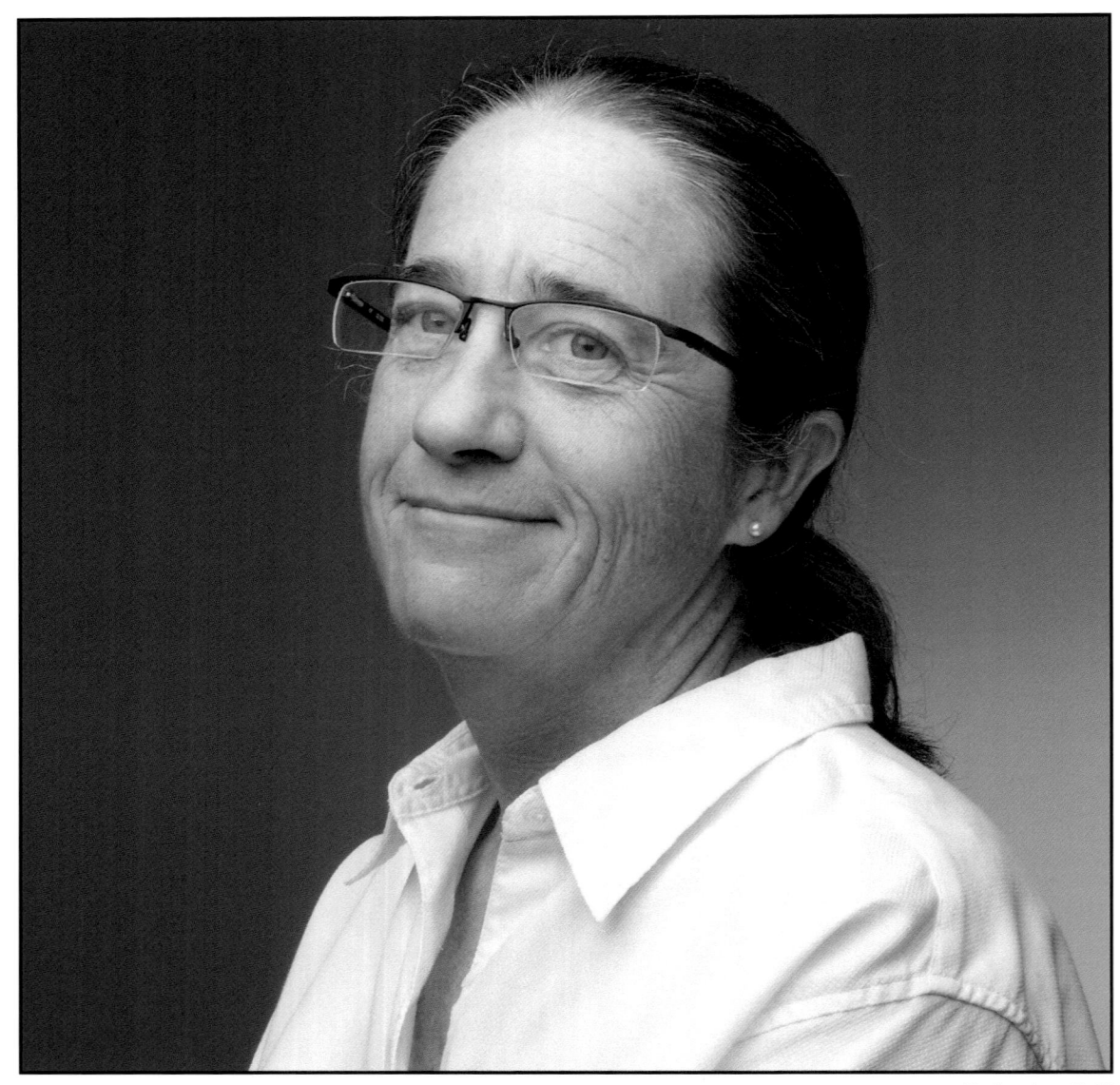

Roberley Bell

the camera seeks

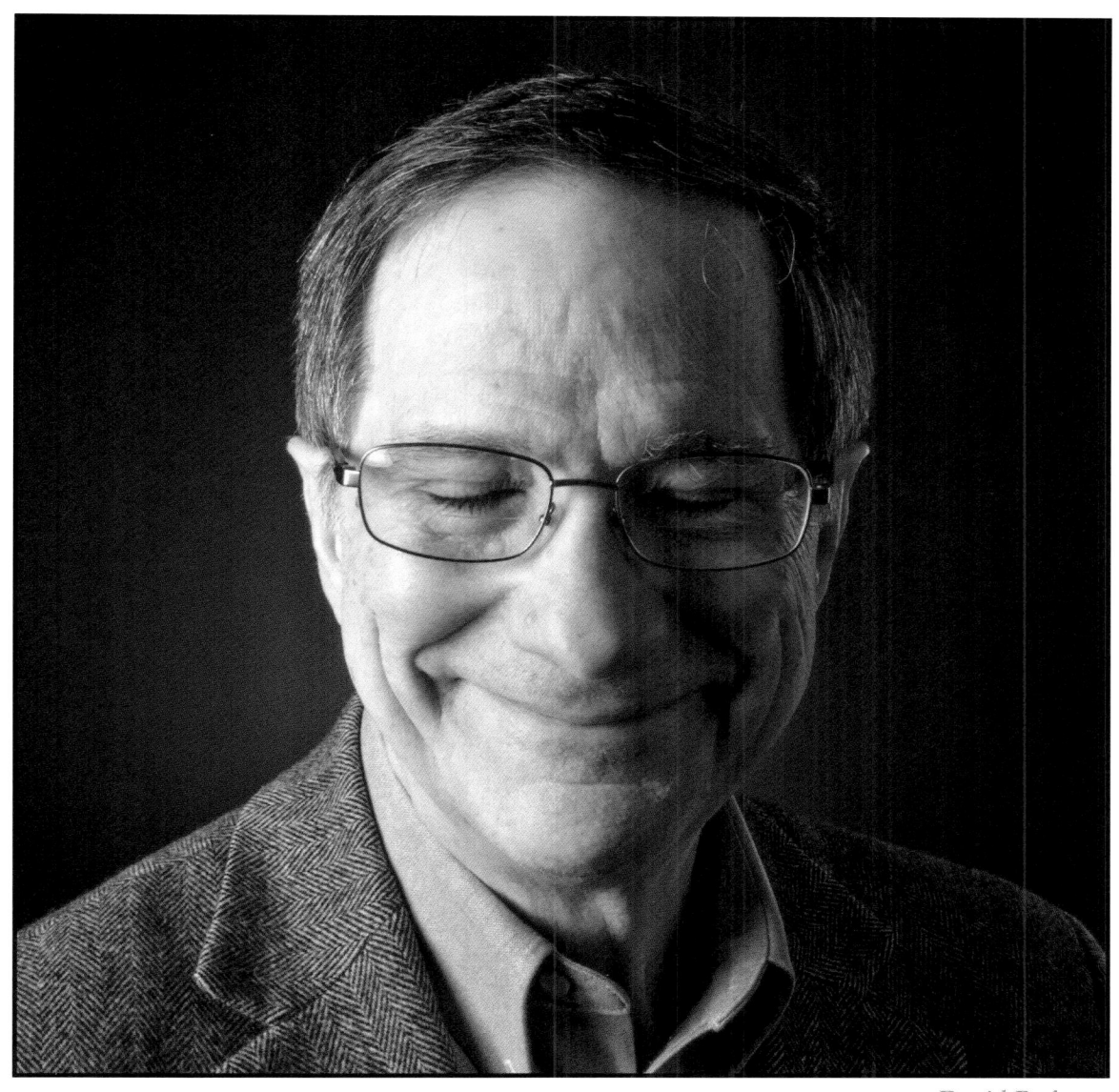

David Perlman

pupil, lid, and lash.

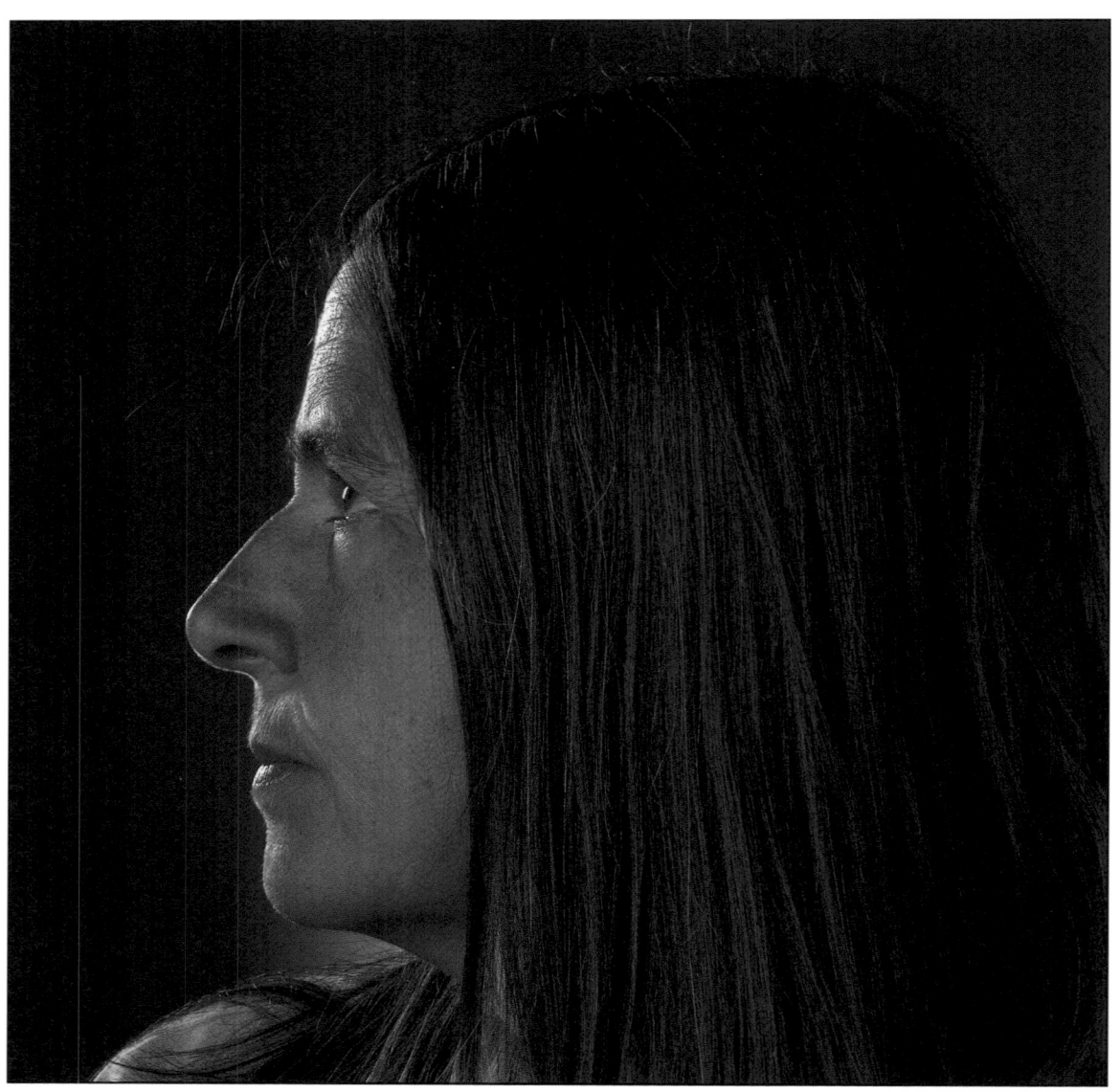

Patricia Albanese Pitkin

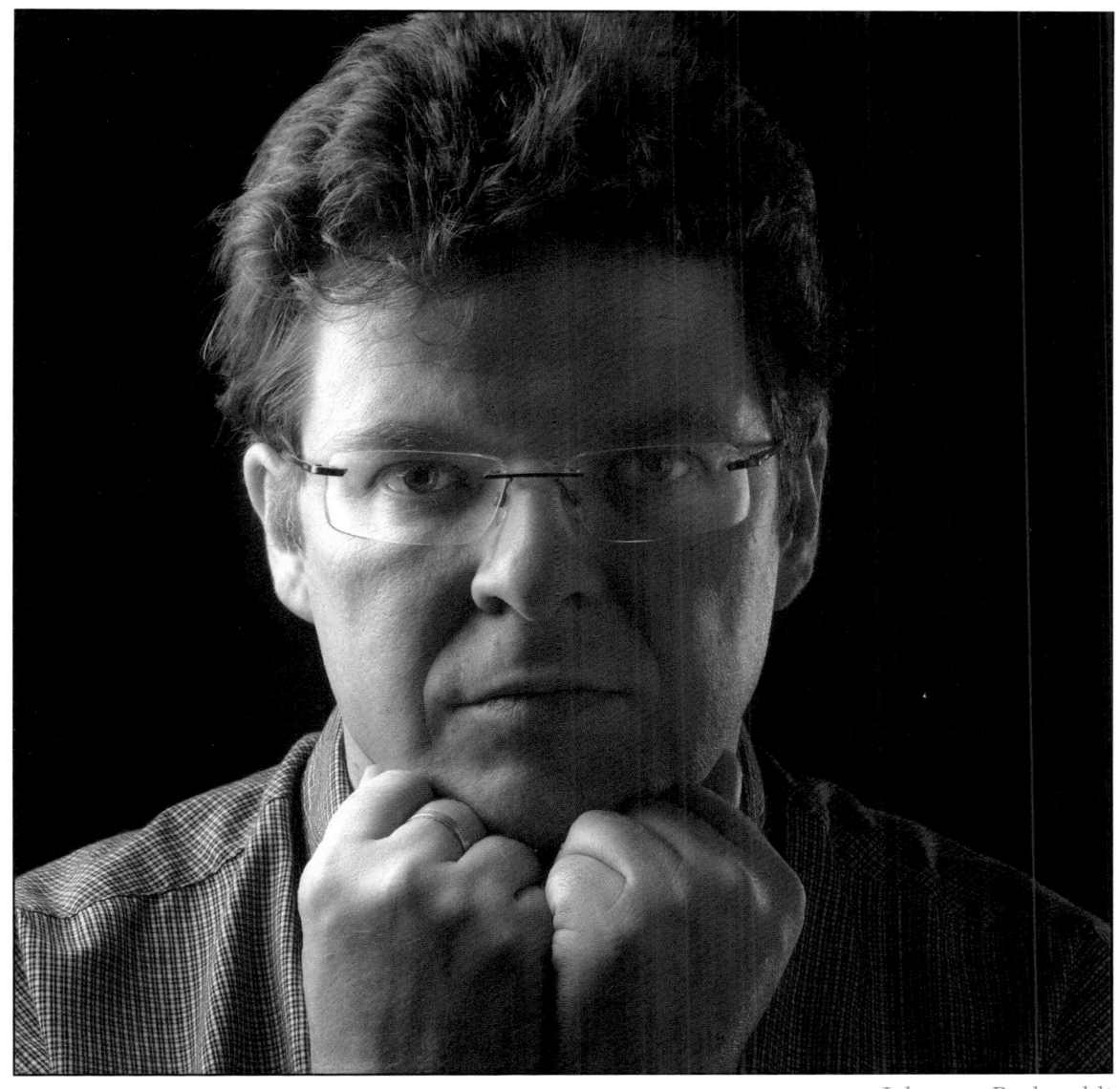

Johannes Bockwoldt

Then enter the eyes

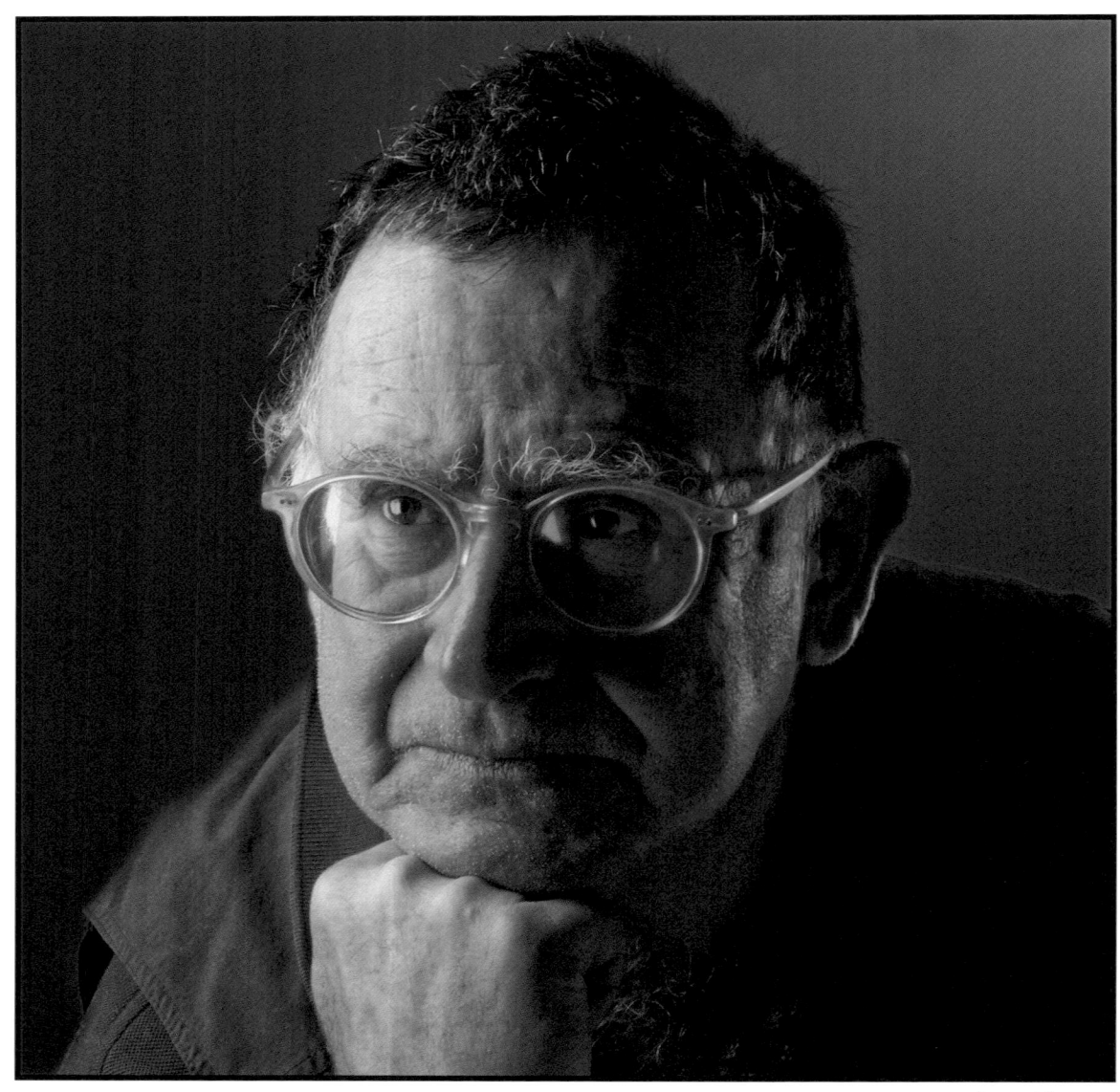

Sam Abrams

bright and black

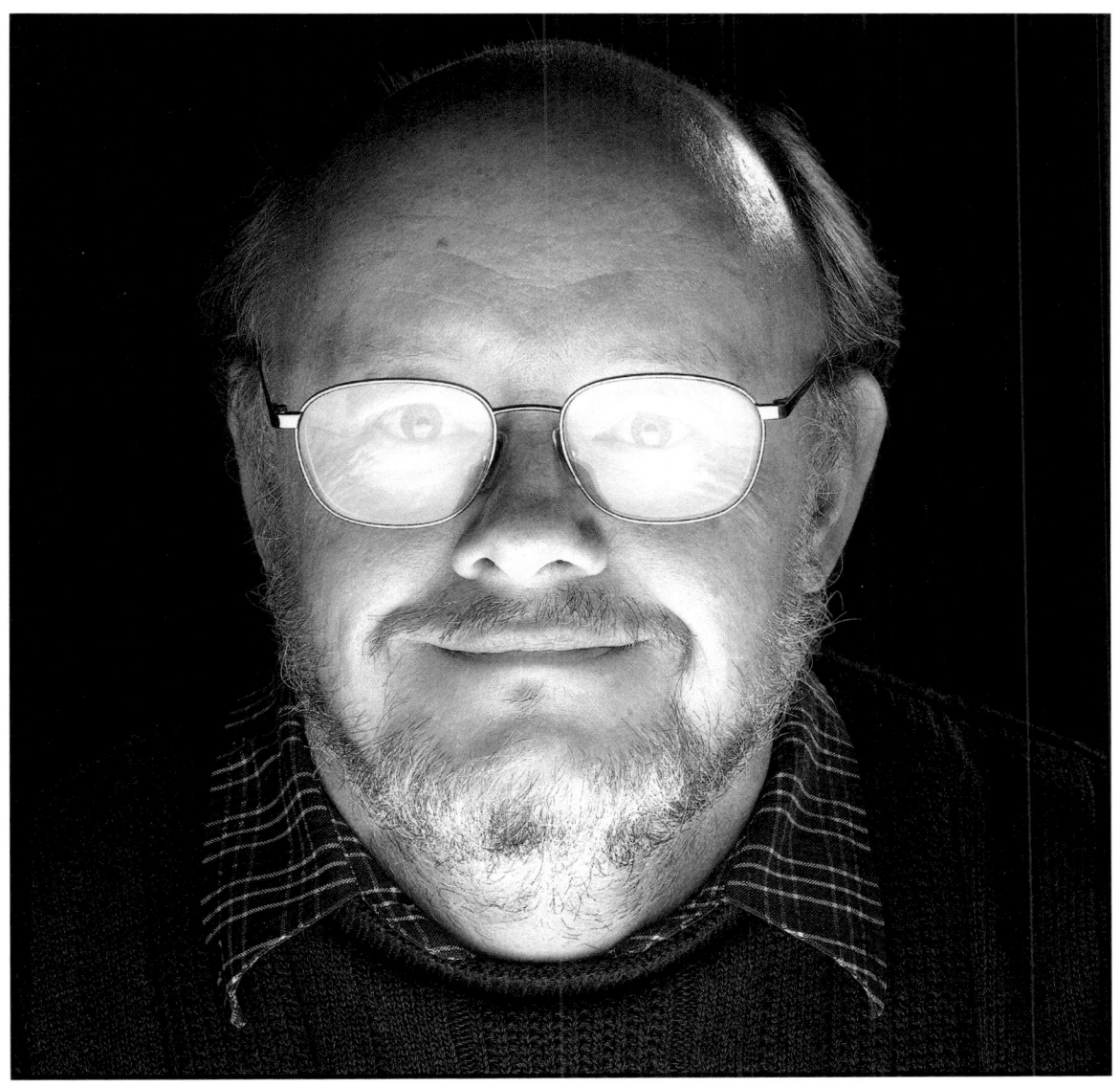

lit from within

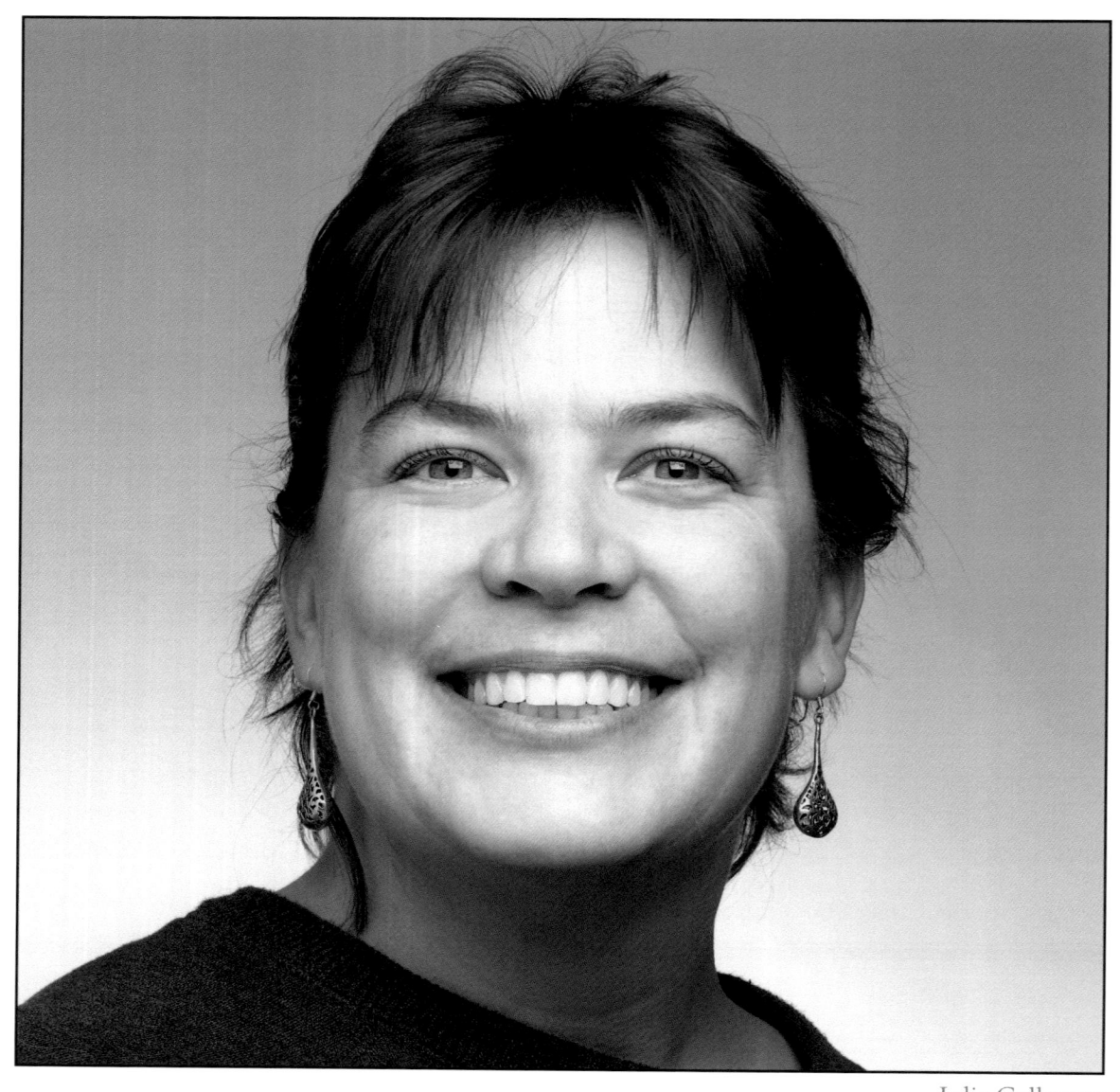

agleam.

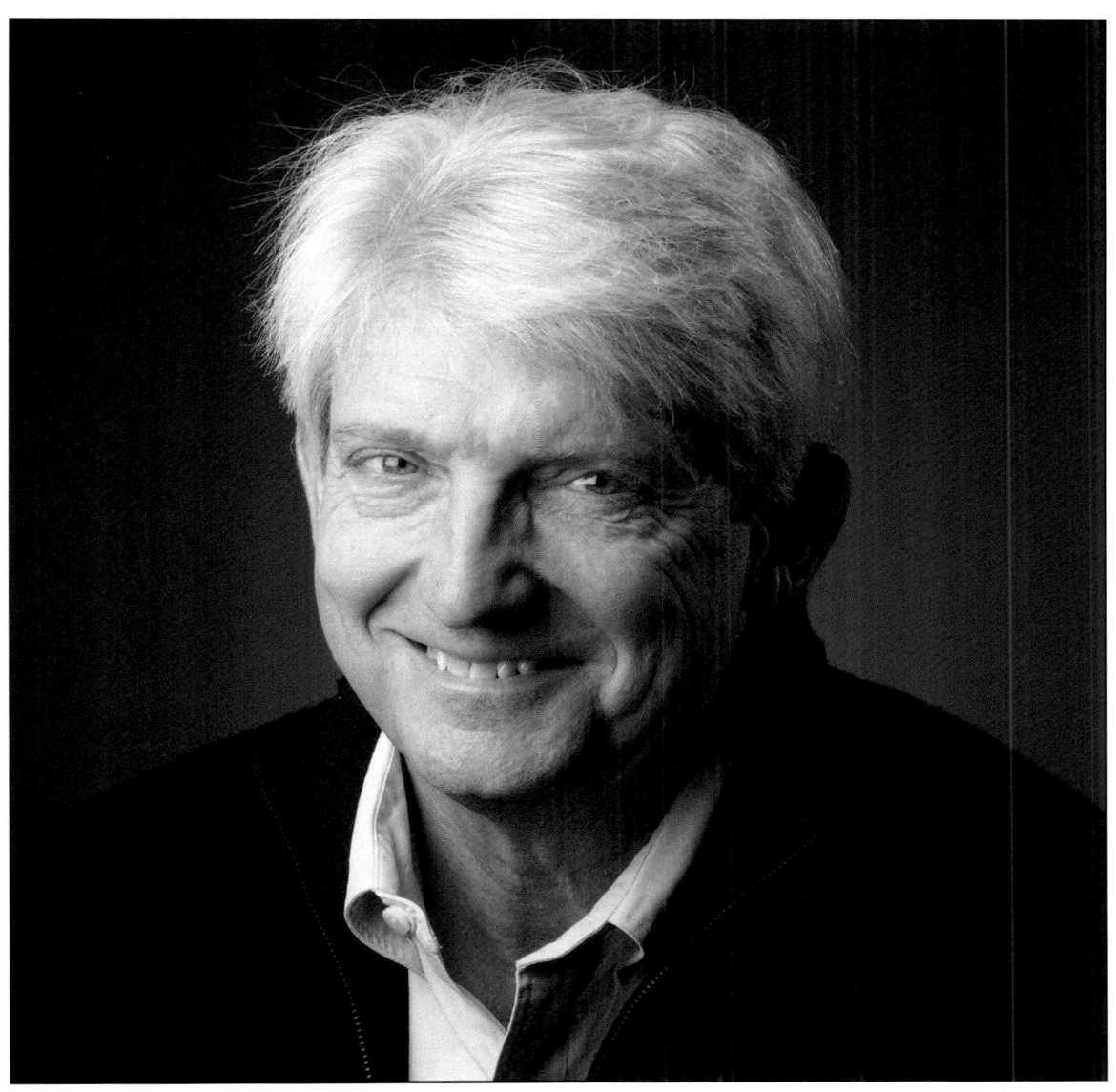

Malcolm Spaull

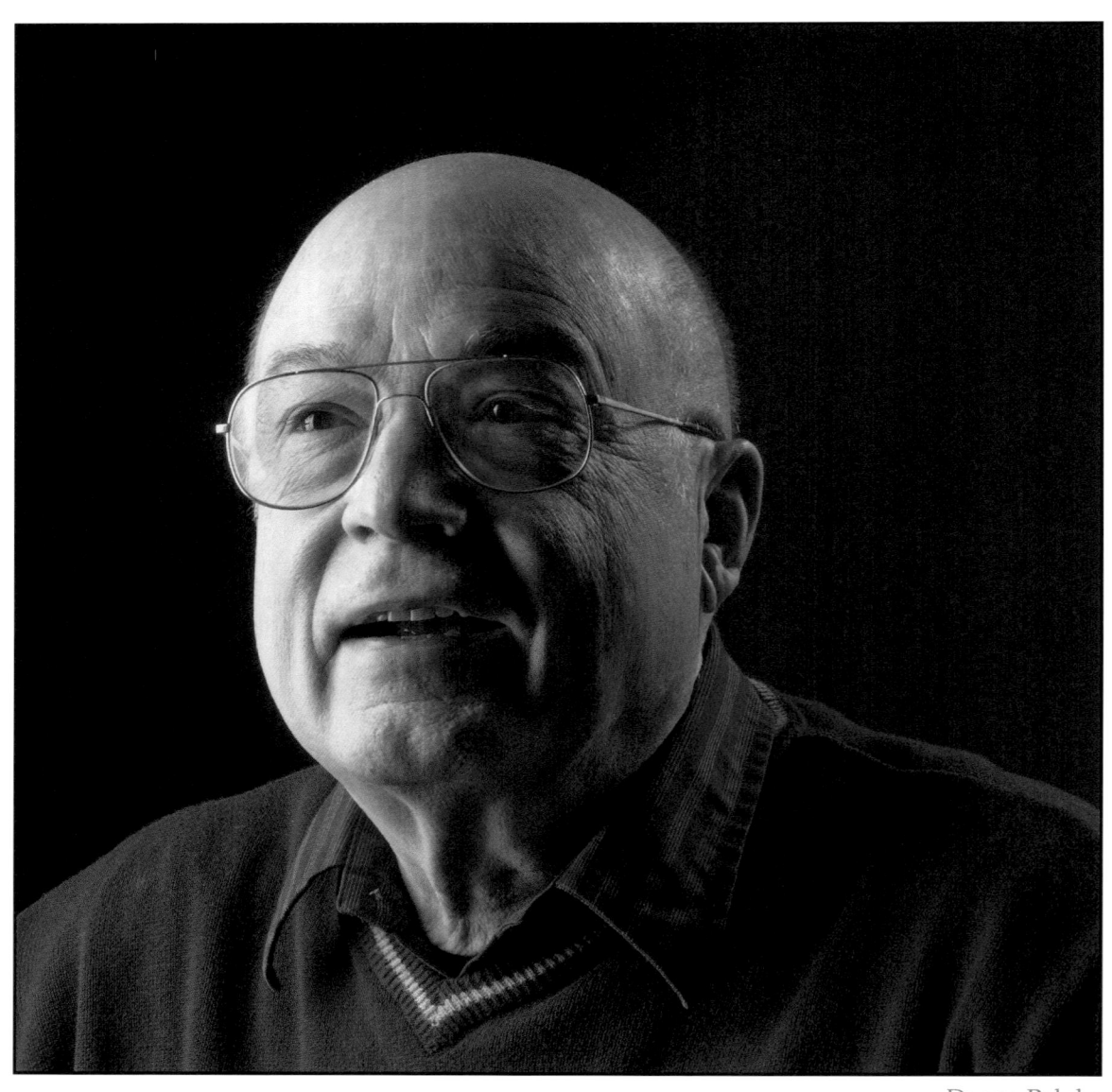

Duane Palyka

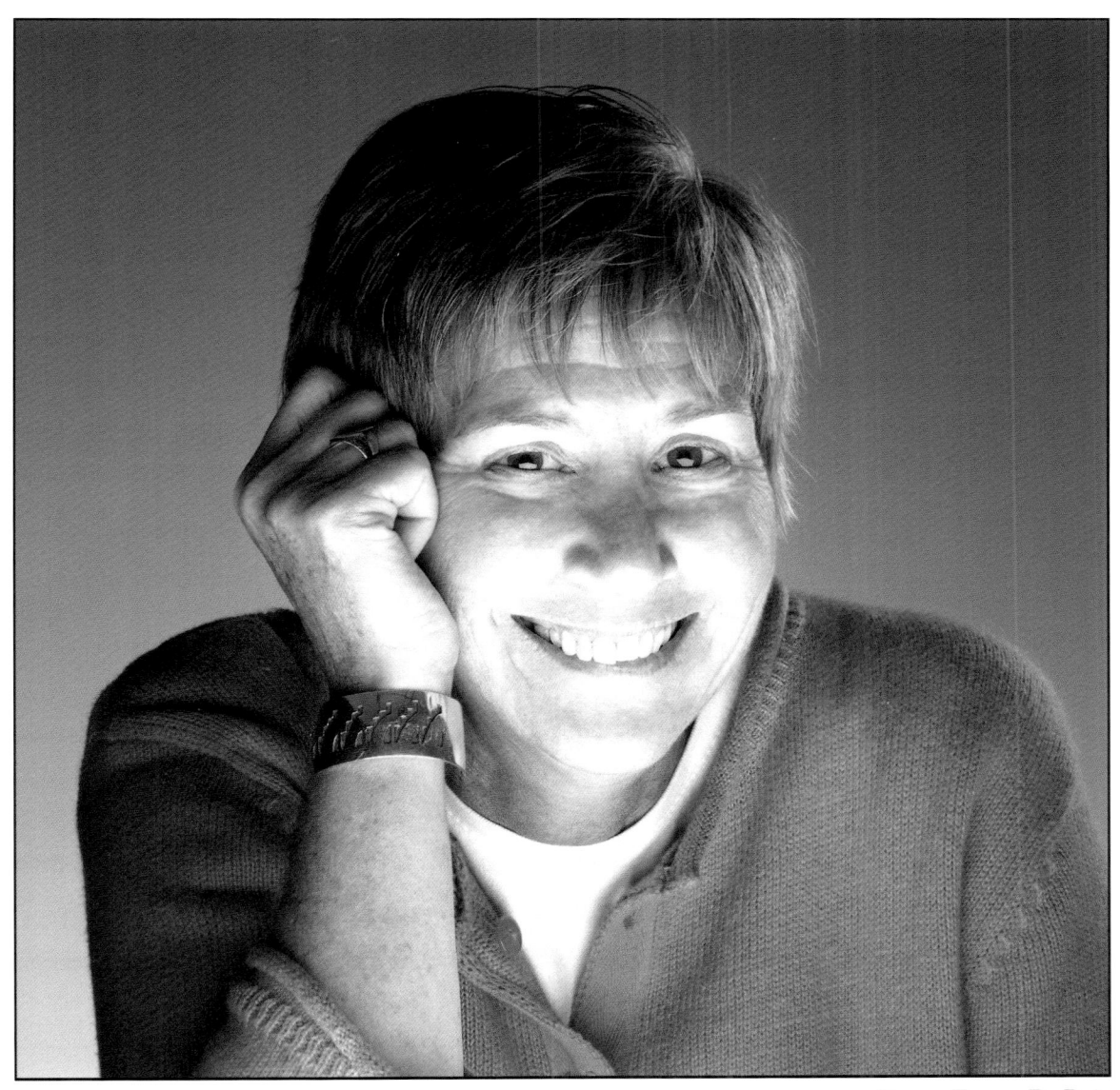

Dawn Tower DuBois

The models beam

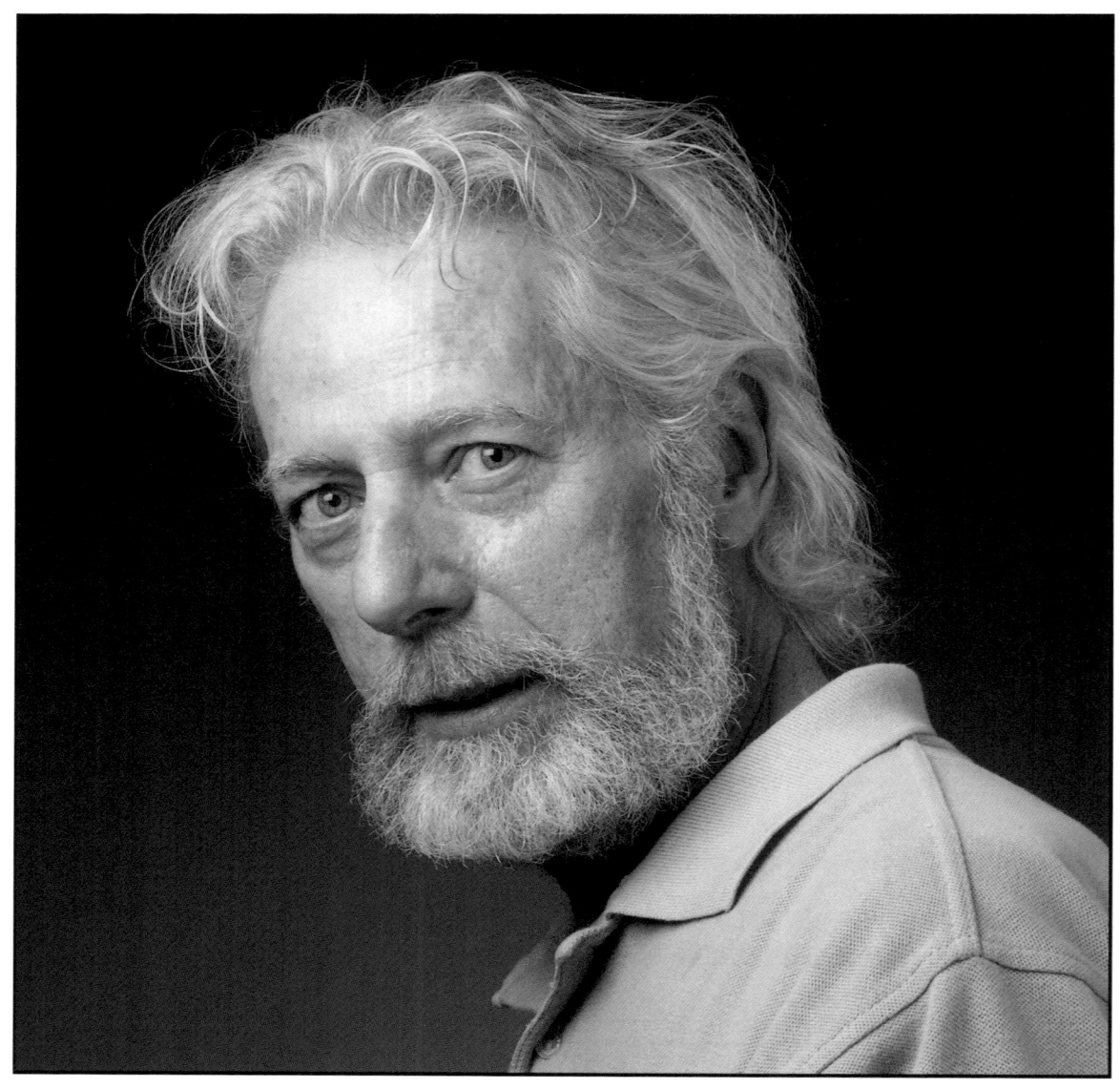

Bob Cole

damp with uneasiness

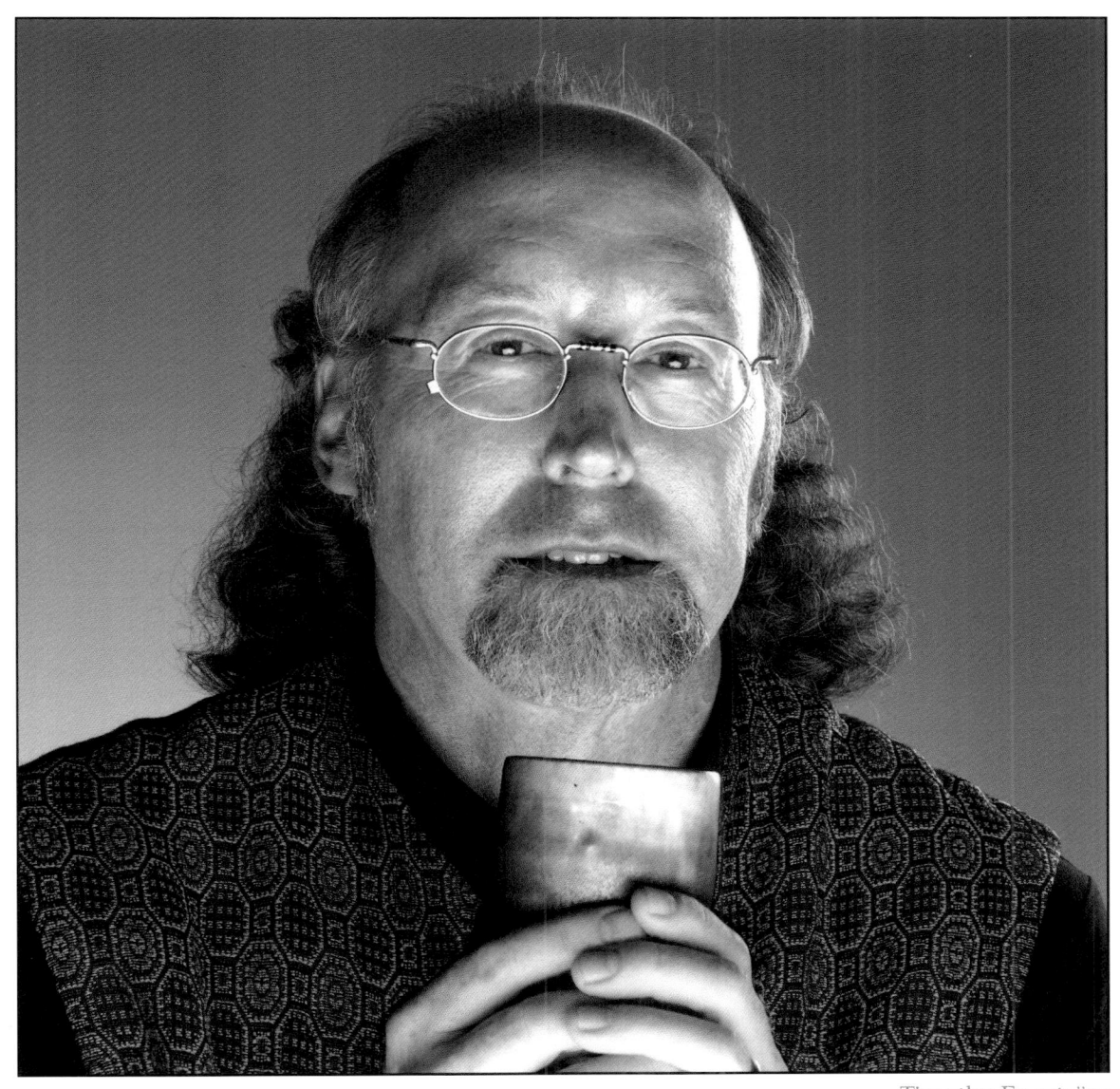

carry props, as if from a treasure box:

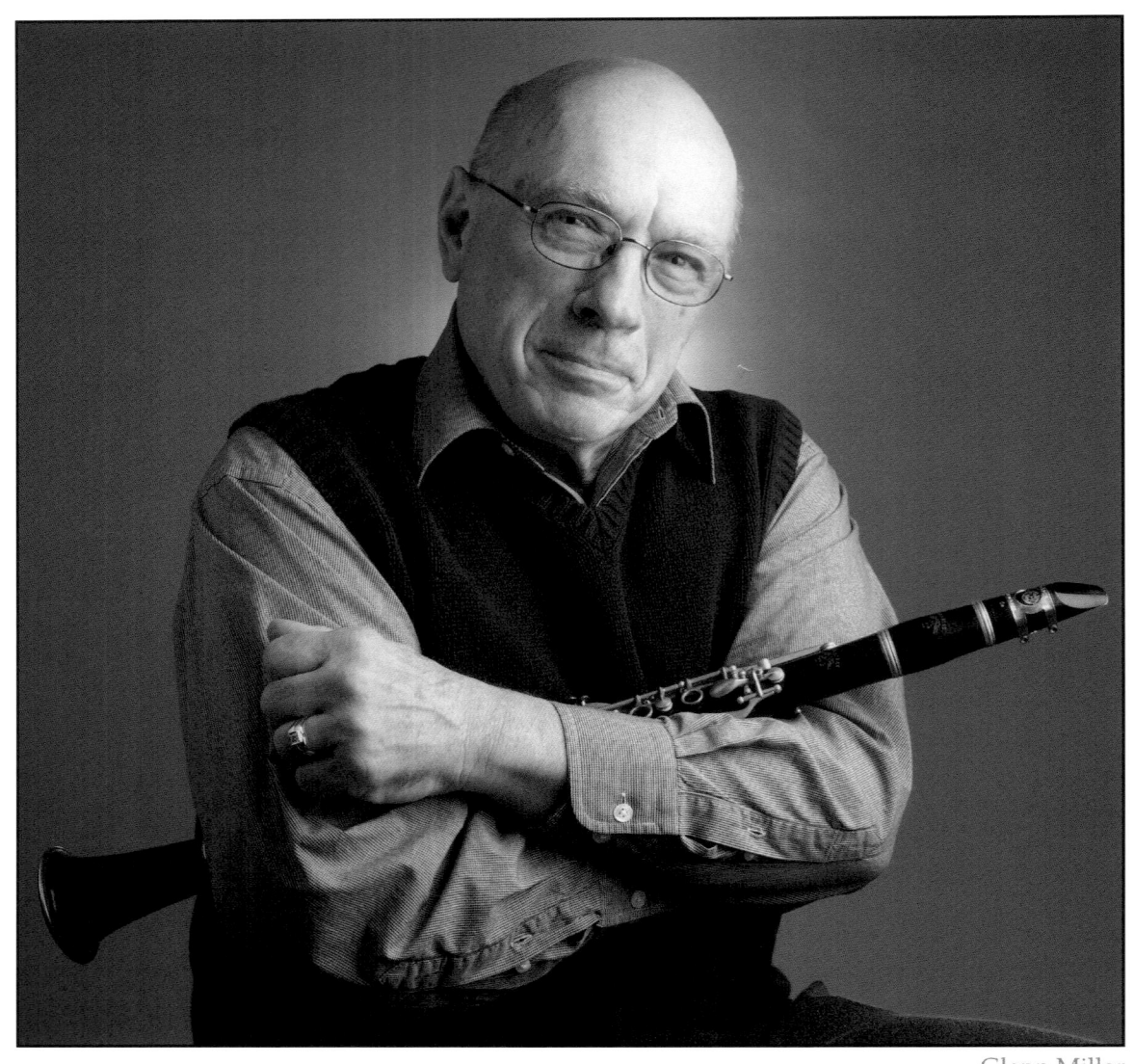

Glenn Miller

clarinet, coffee cup, beads of stone.

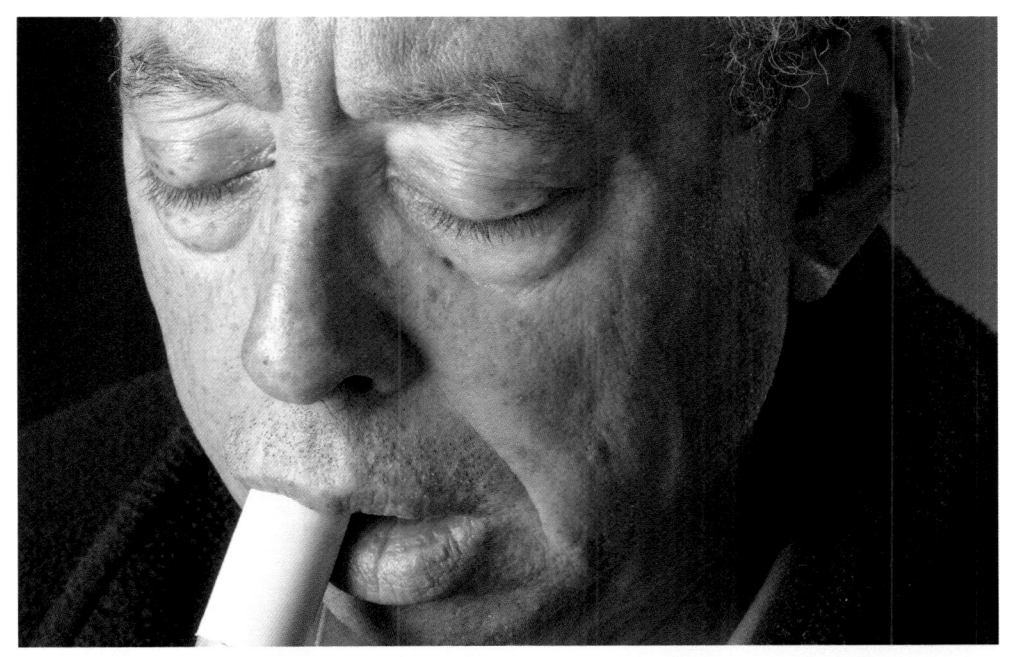

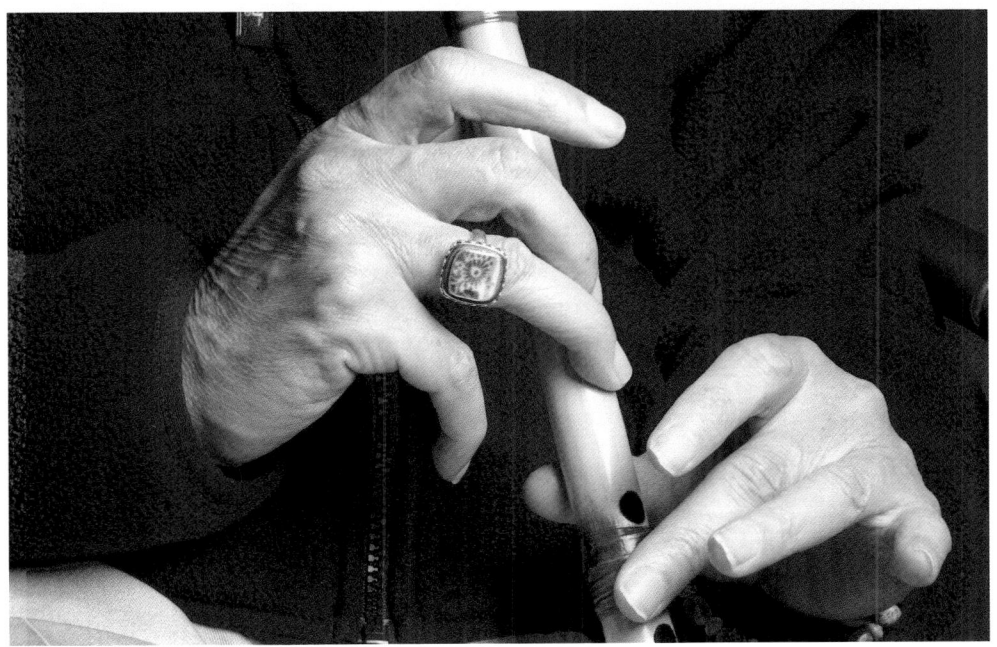

Owen Butler

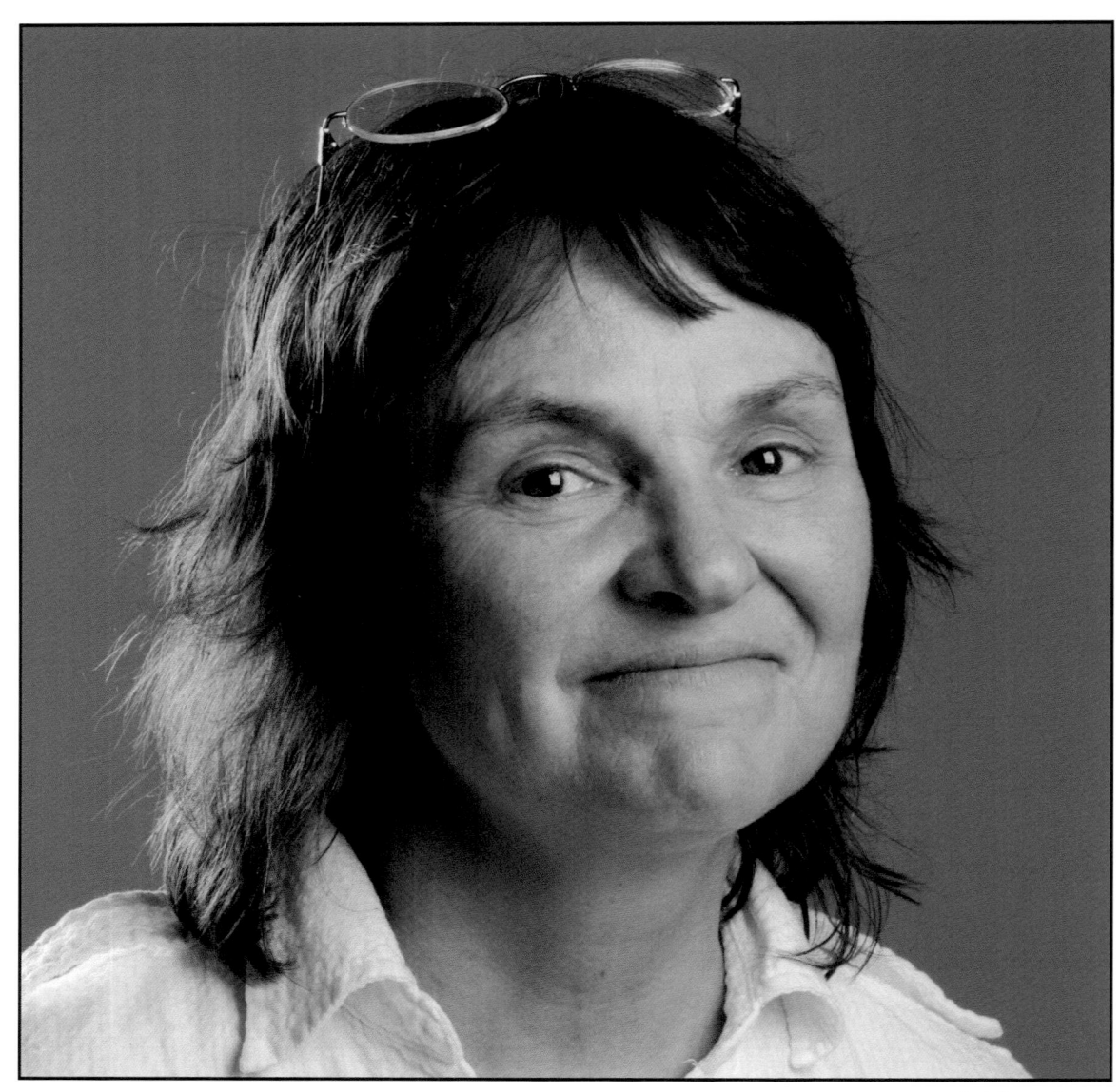

Patti Ambrogi

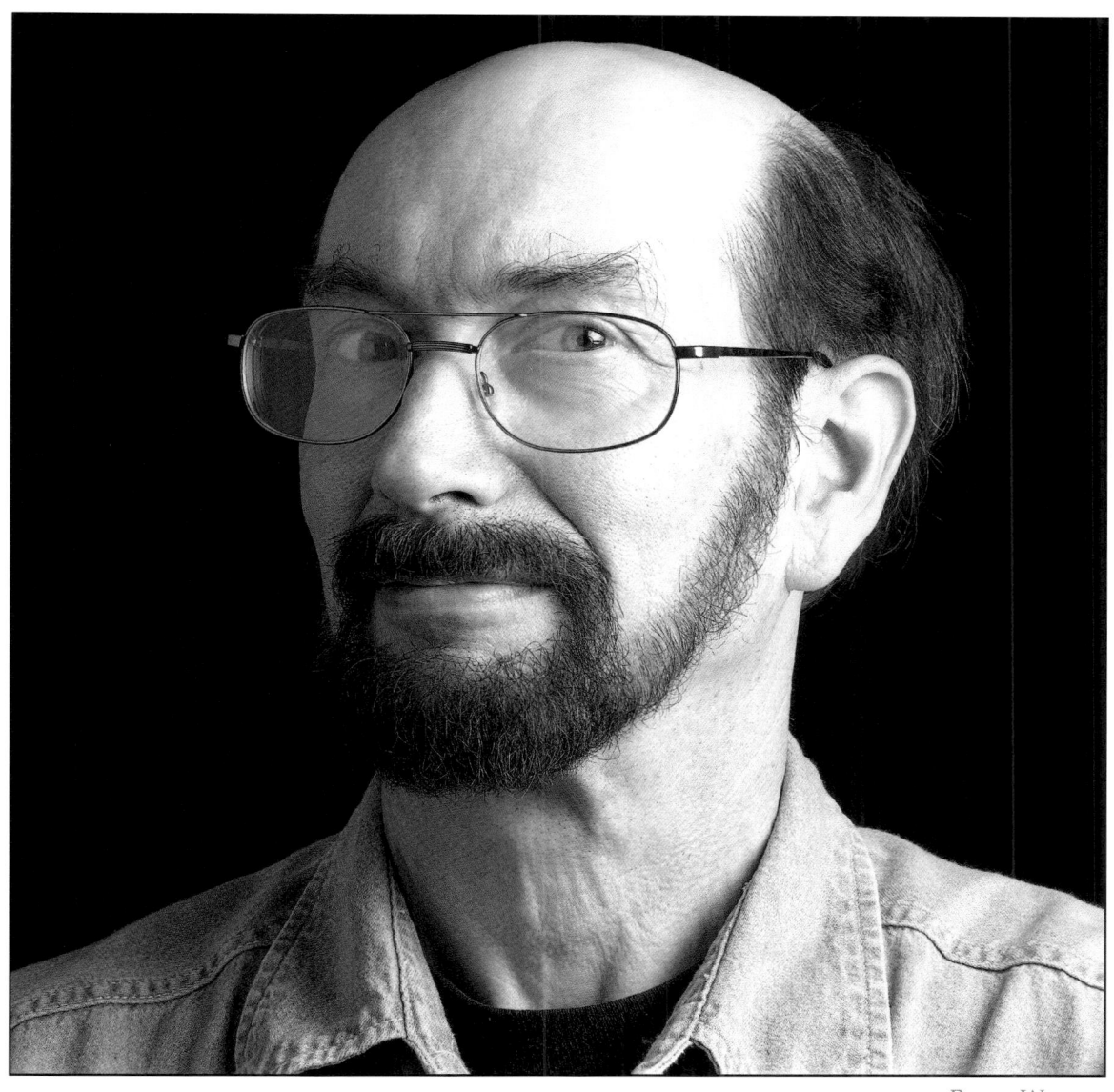

Bruce Wenger

Enter the eyes

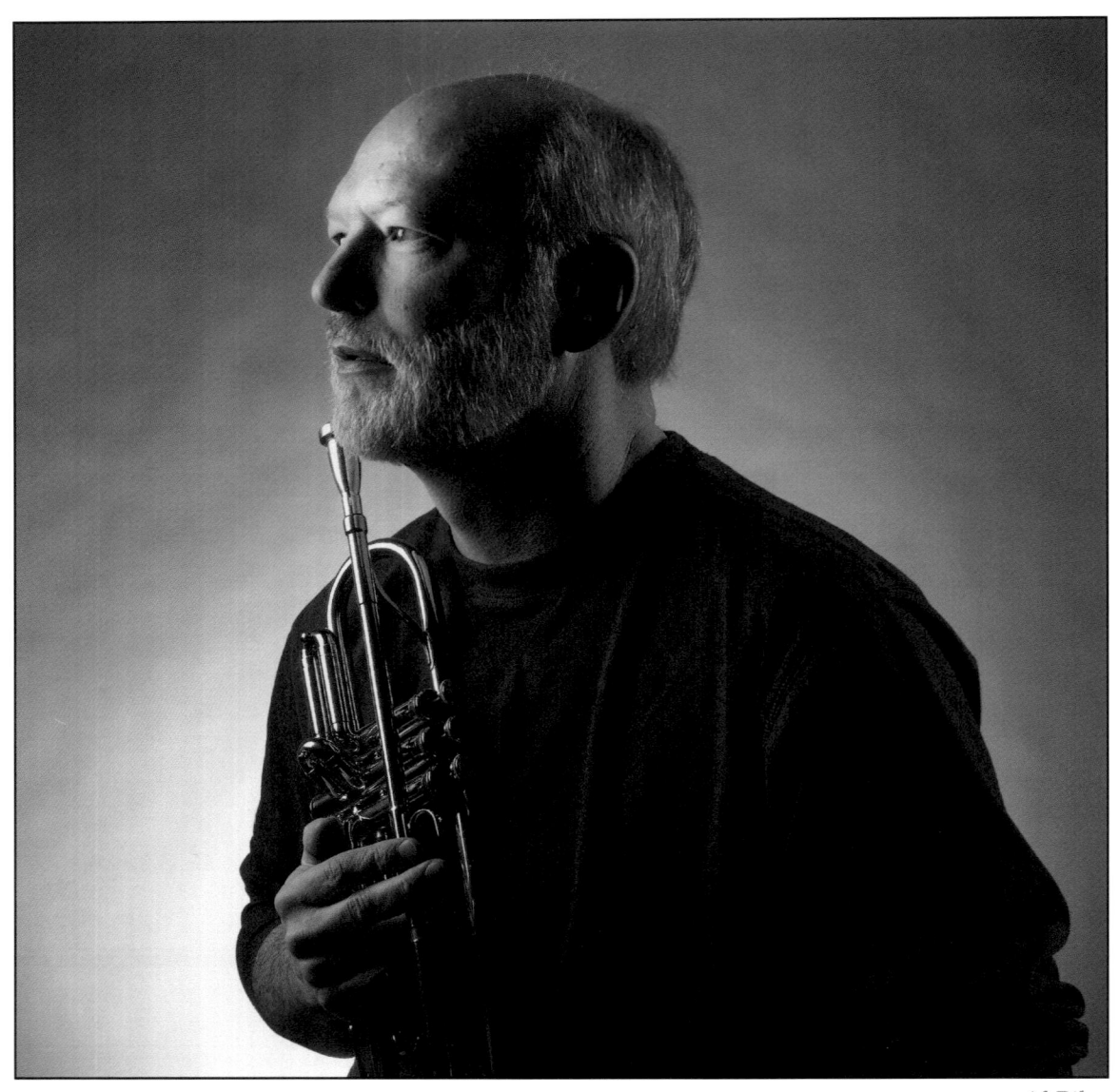

Al Biles

of those who make music

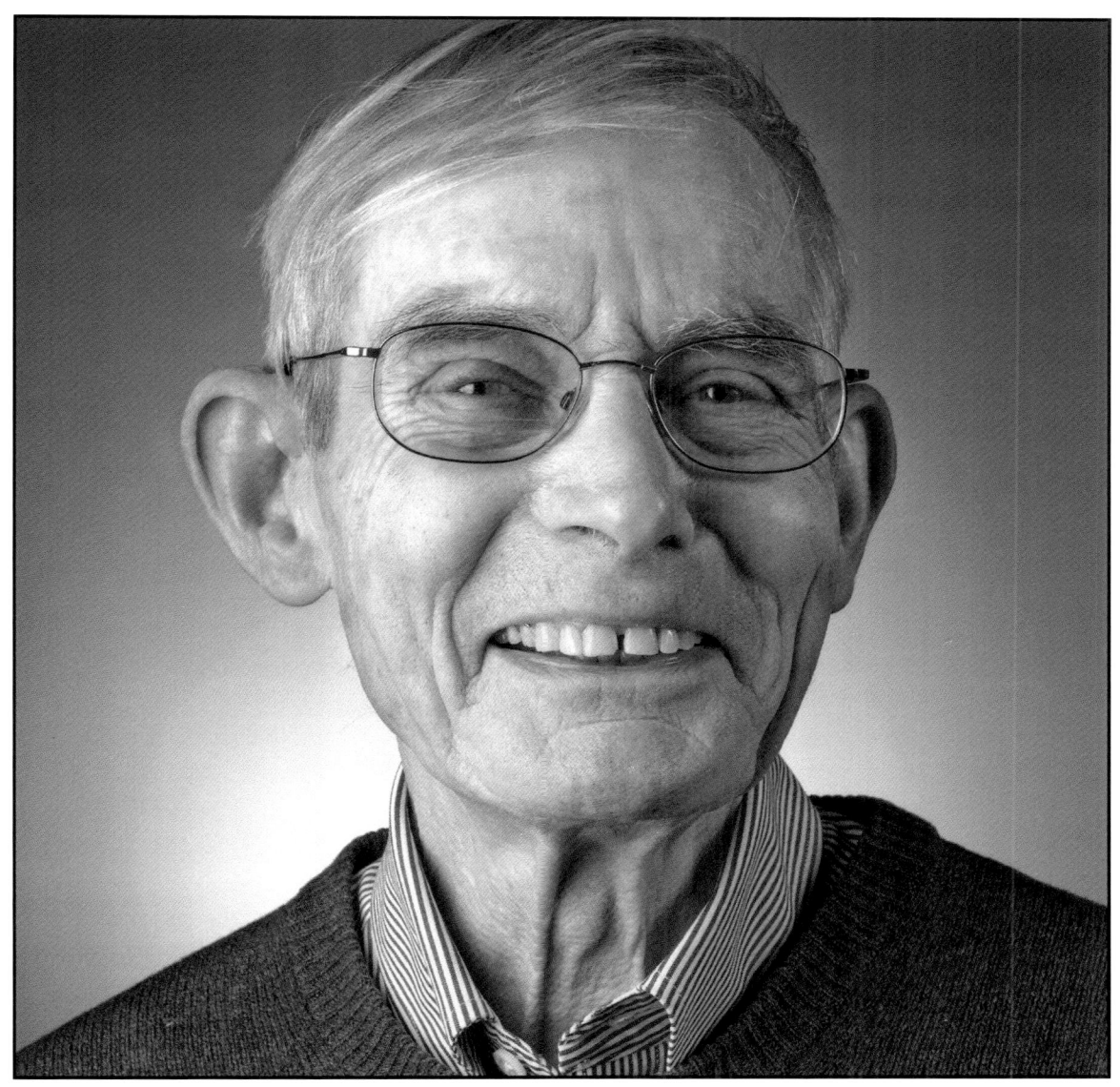

Dane Gordon

bend light and words

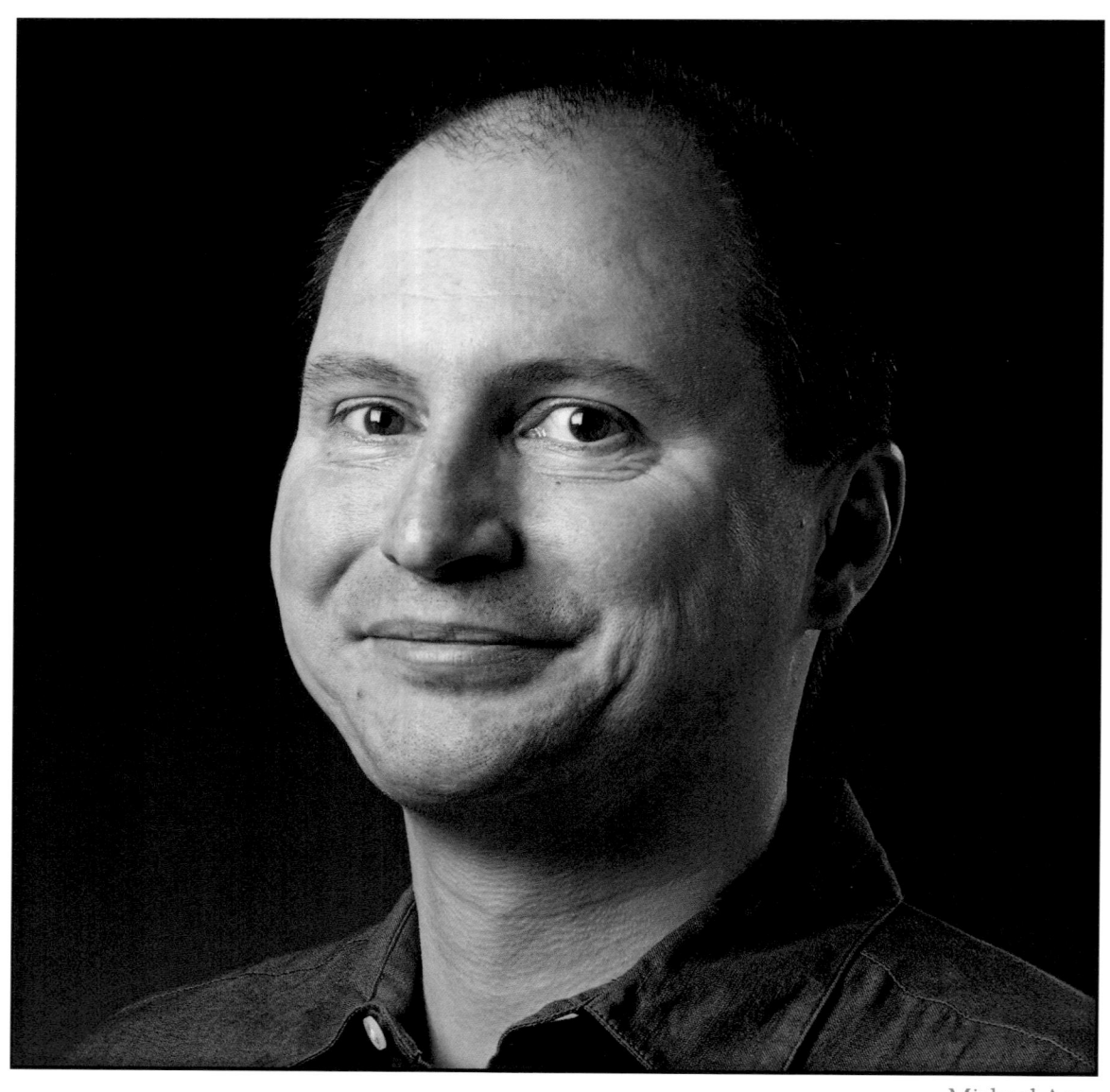

Michael Amy

send ideas soaring.

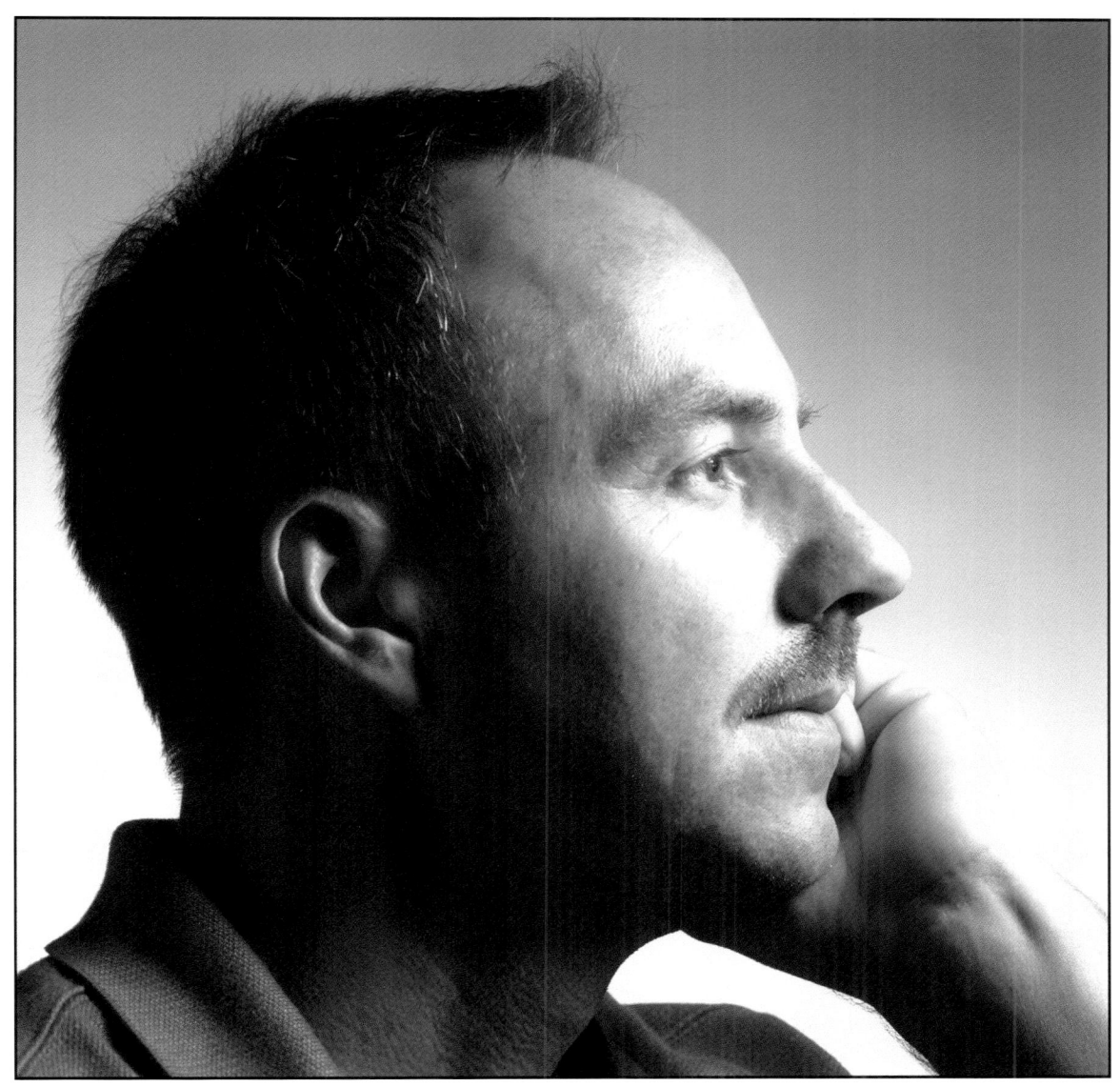

Mike Dear

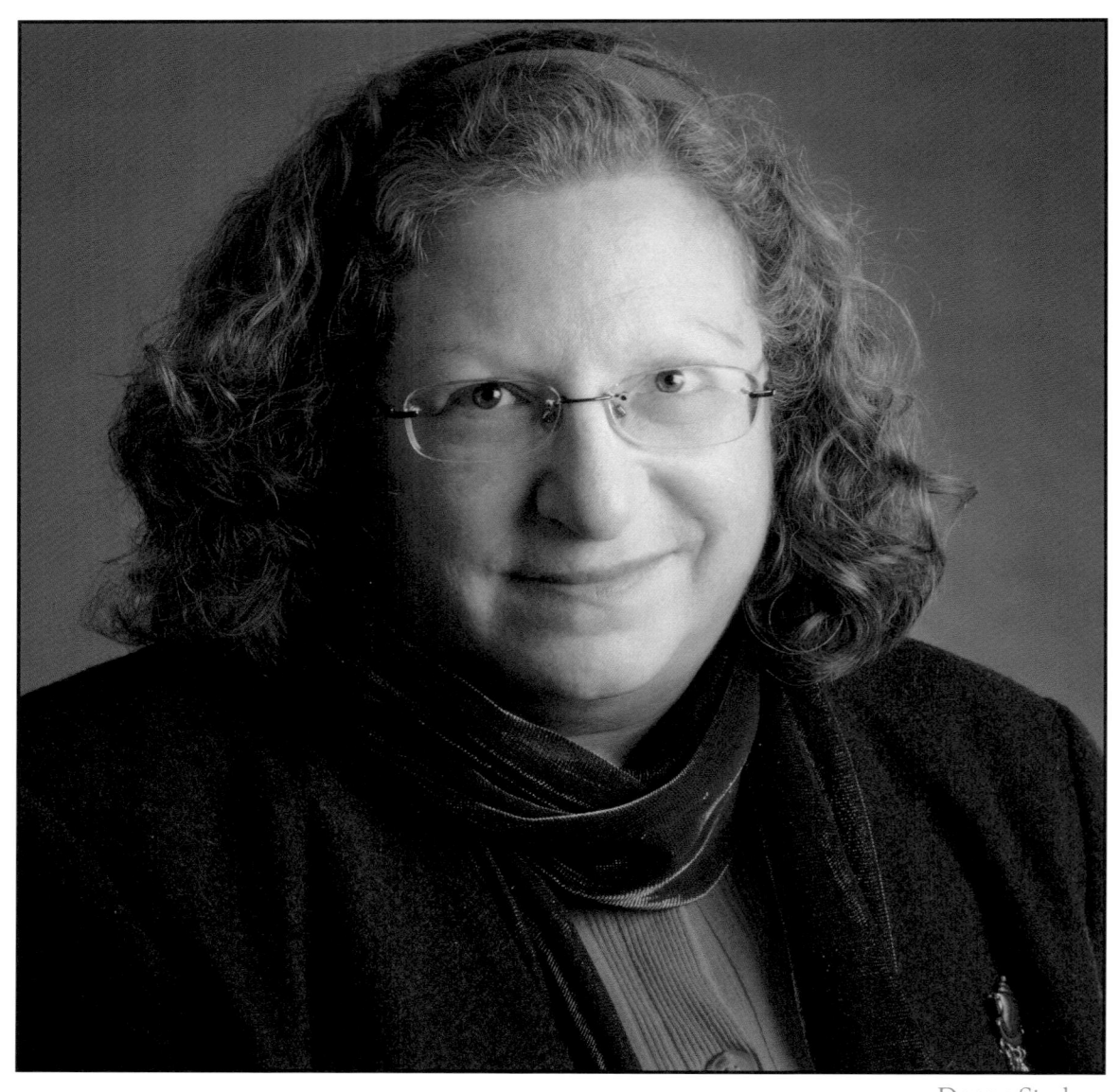

Donna Sterlace

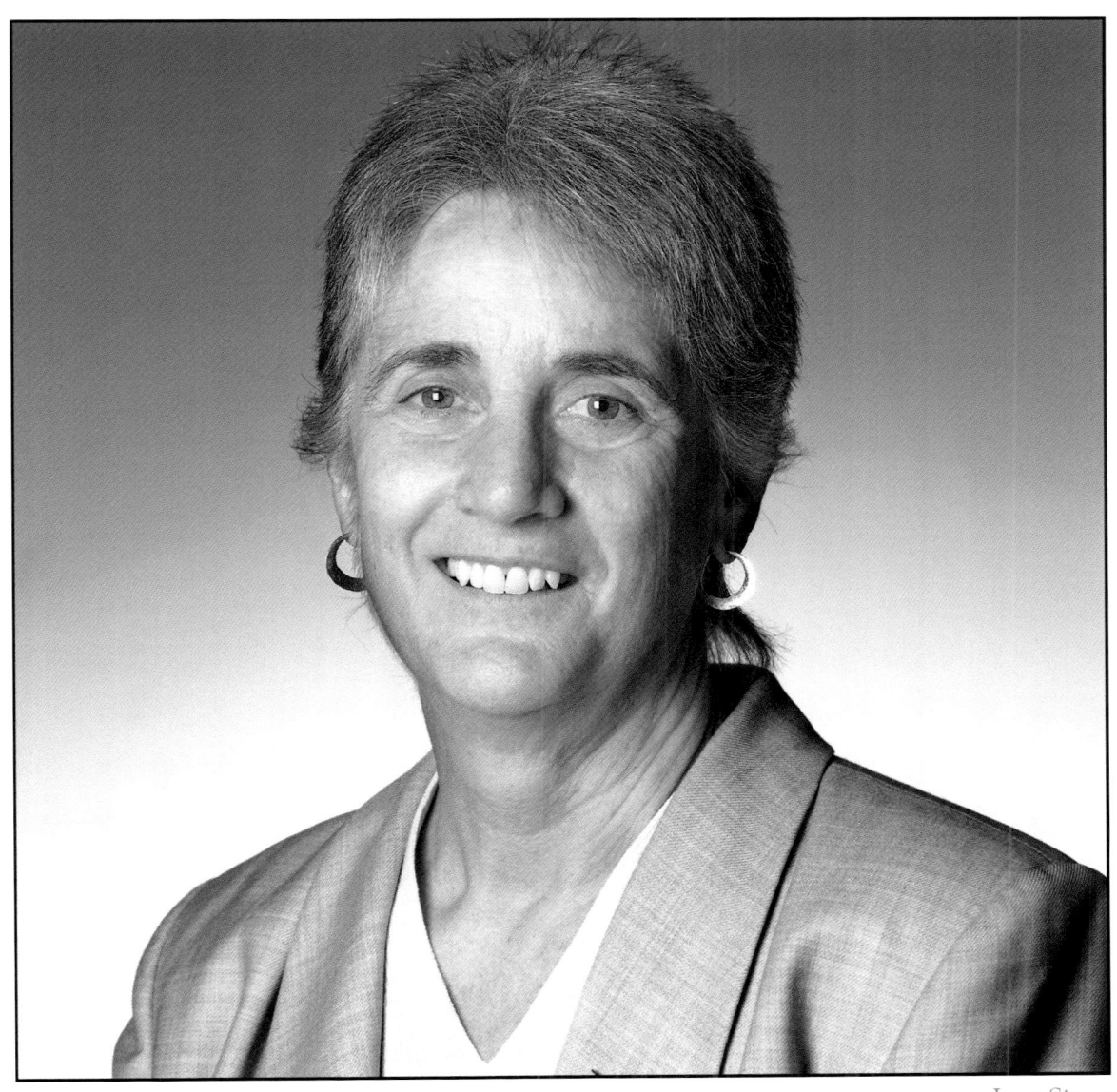

Joan Stone

Teased out, unguarded,

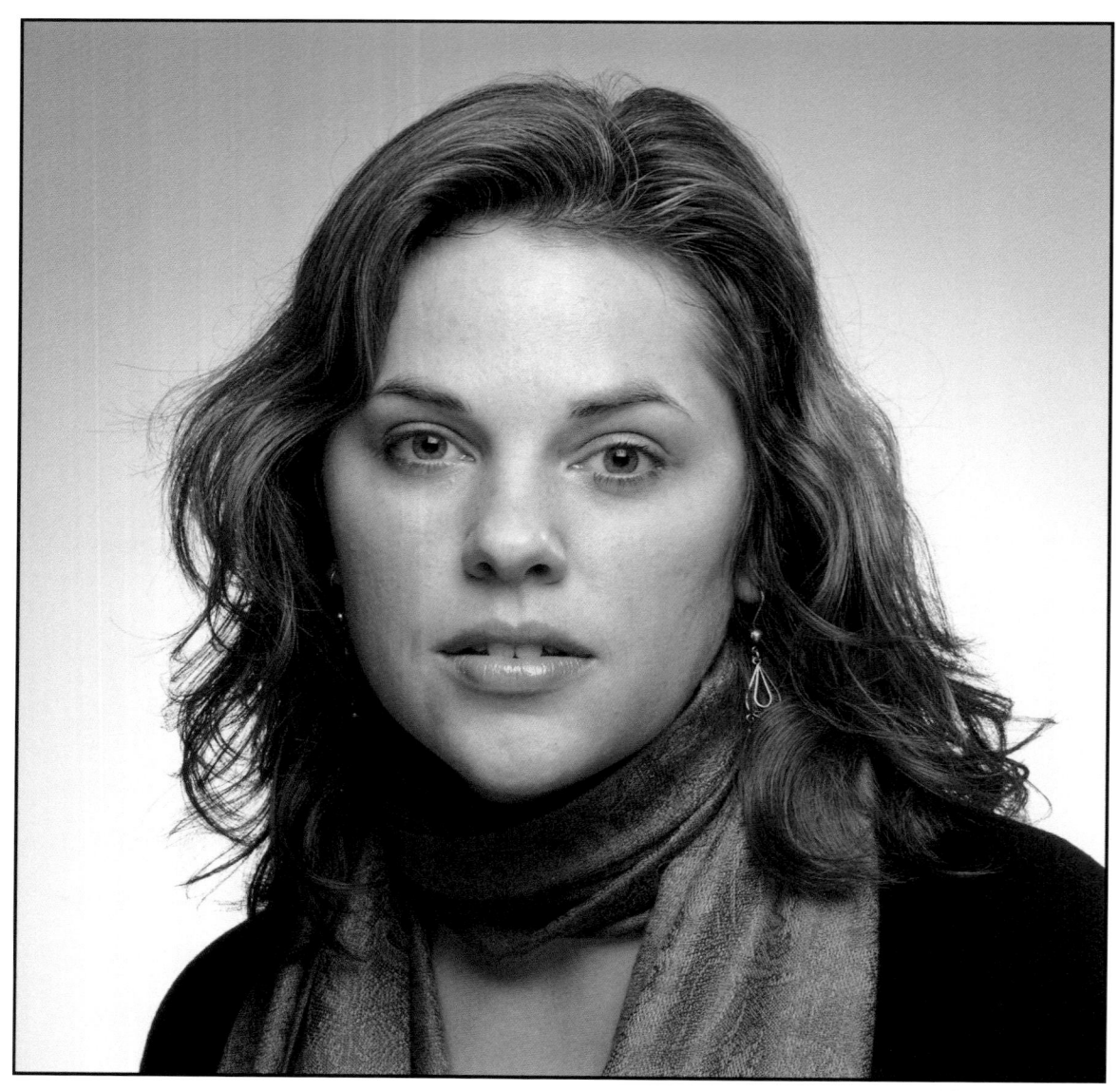

they become

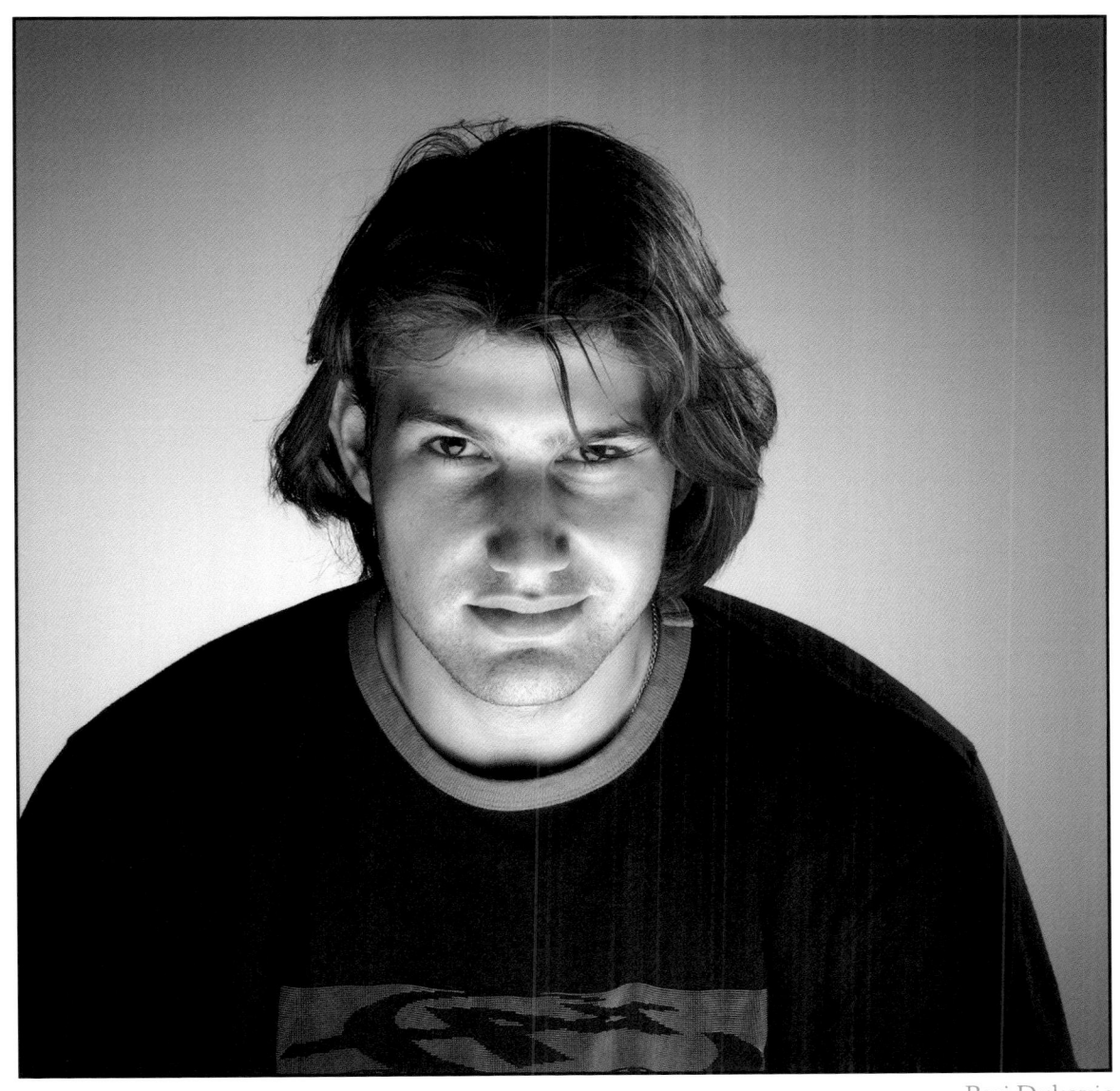

Pari Dukovic

images of themselves

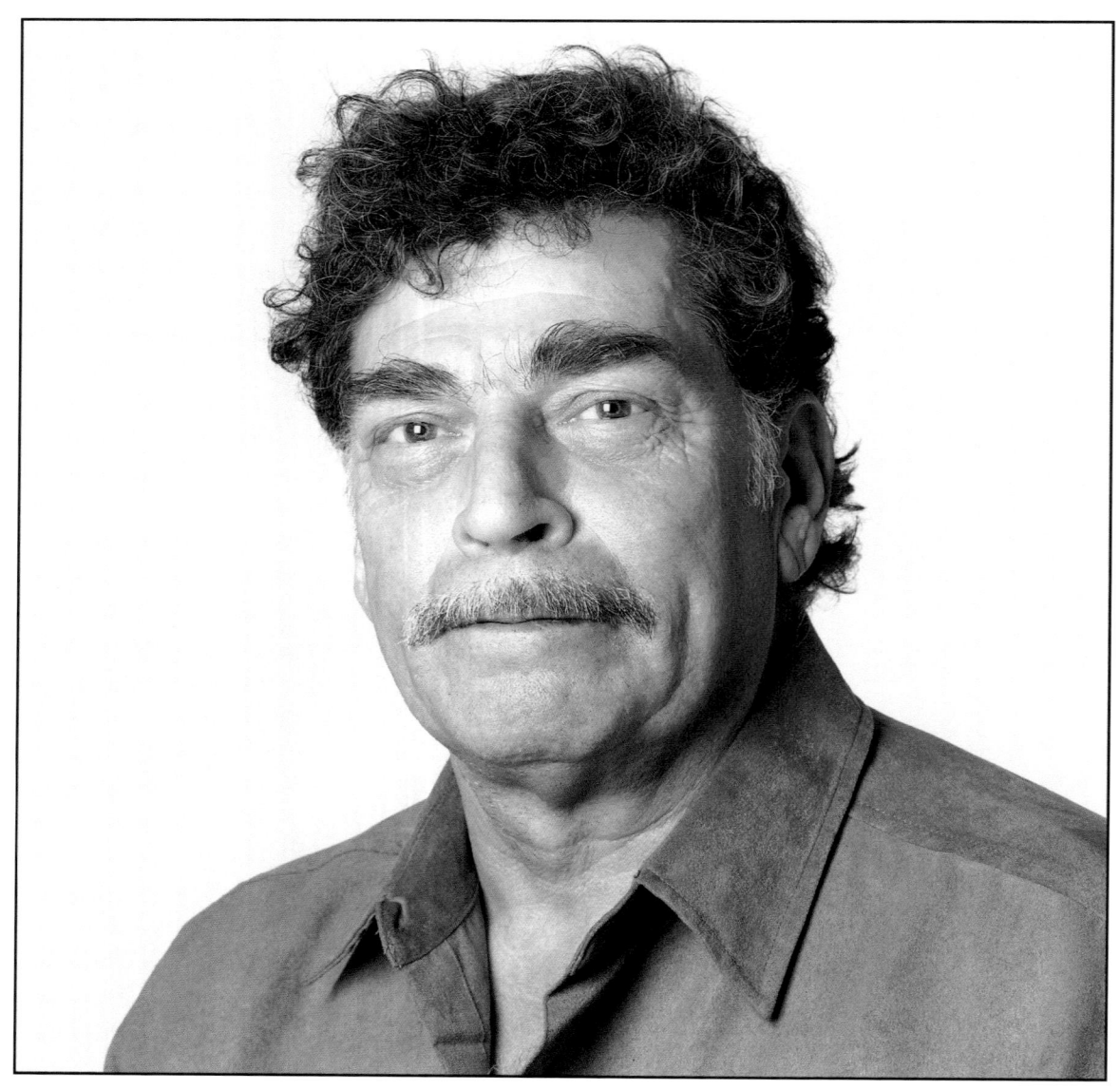

Howard Lester

stories, melodies

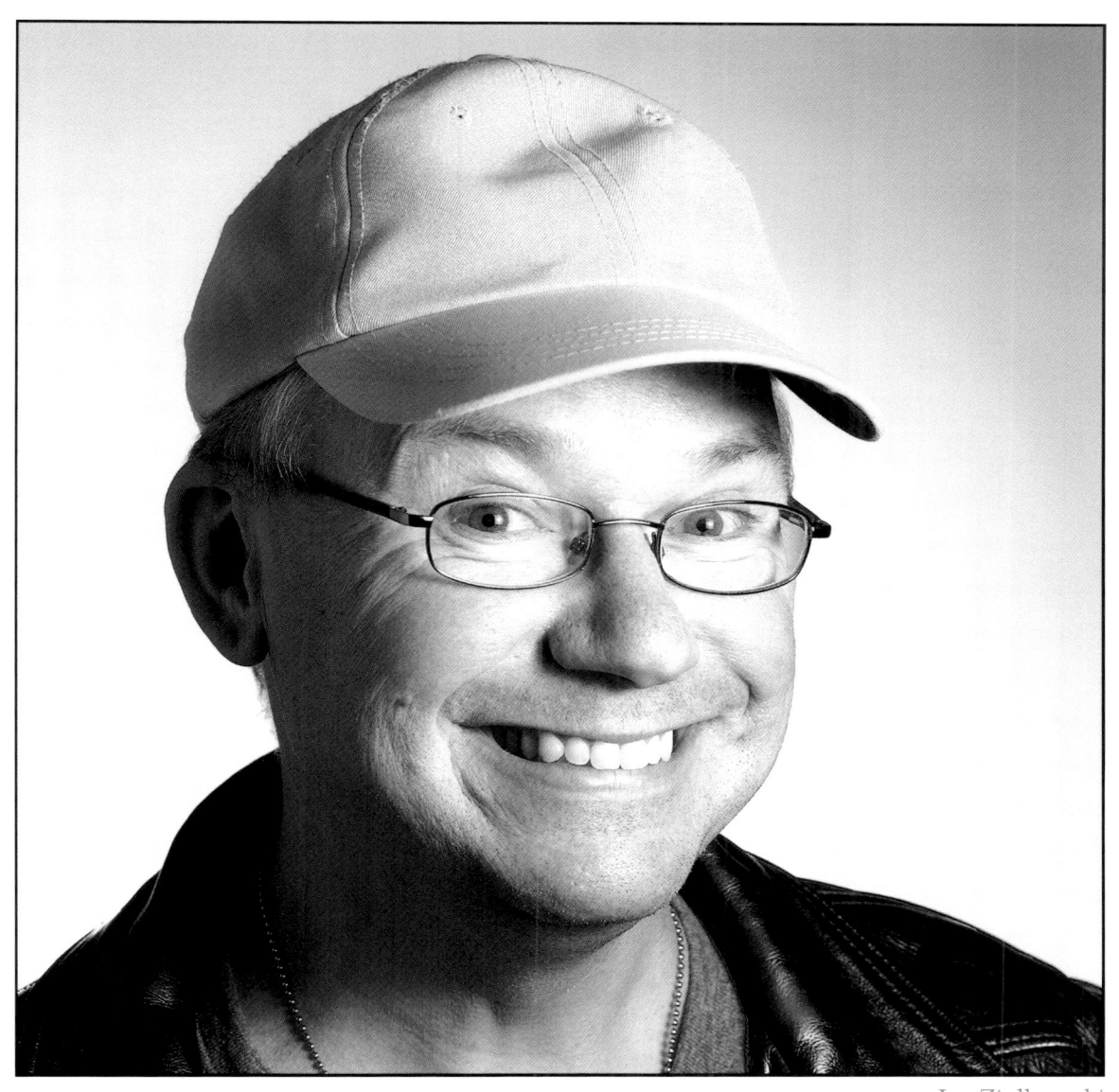

Joe Ziolkowski

pressed to the page.

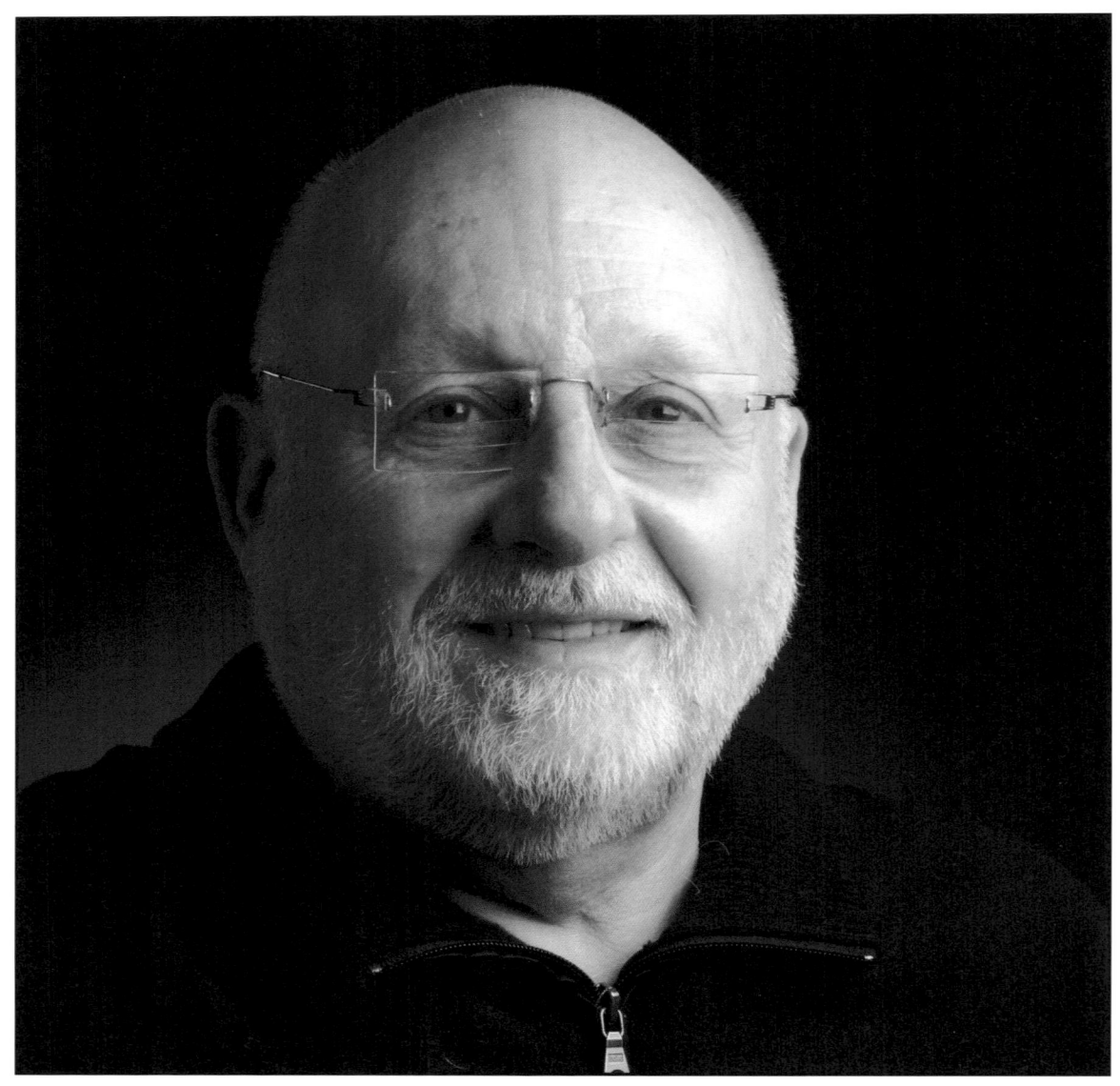

Roger Remington

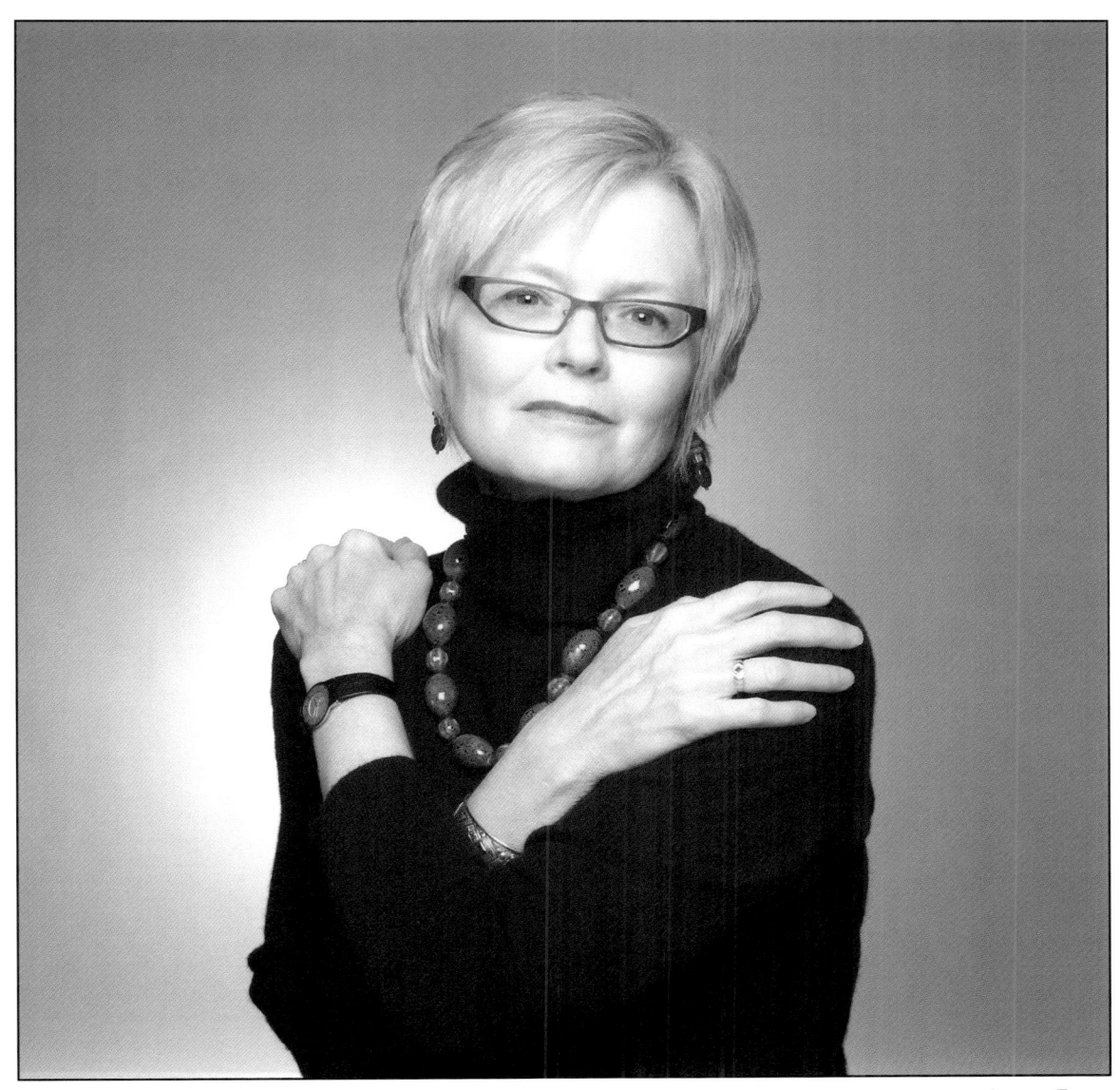

Anne Coon

Enter the eyes of women and men

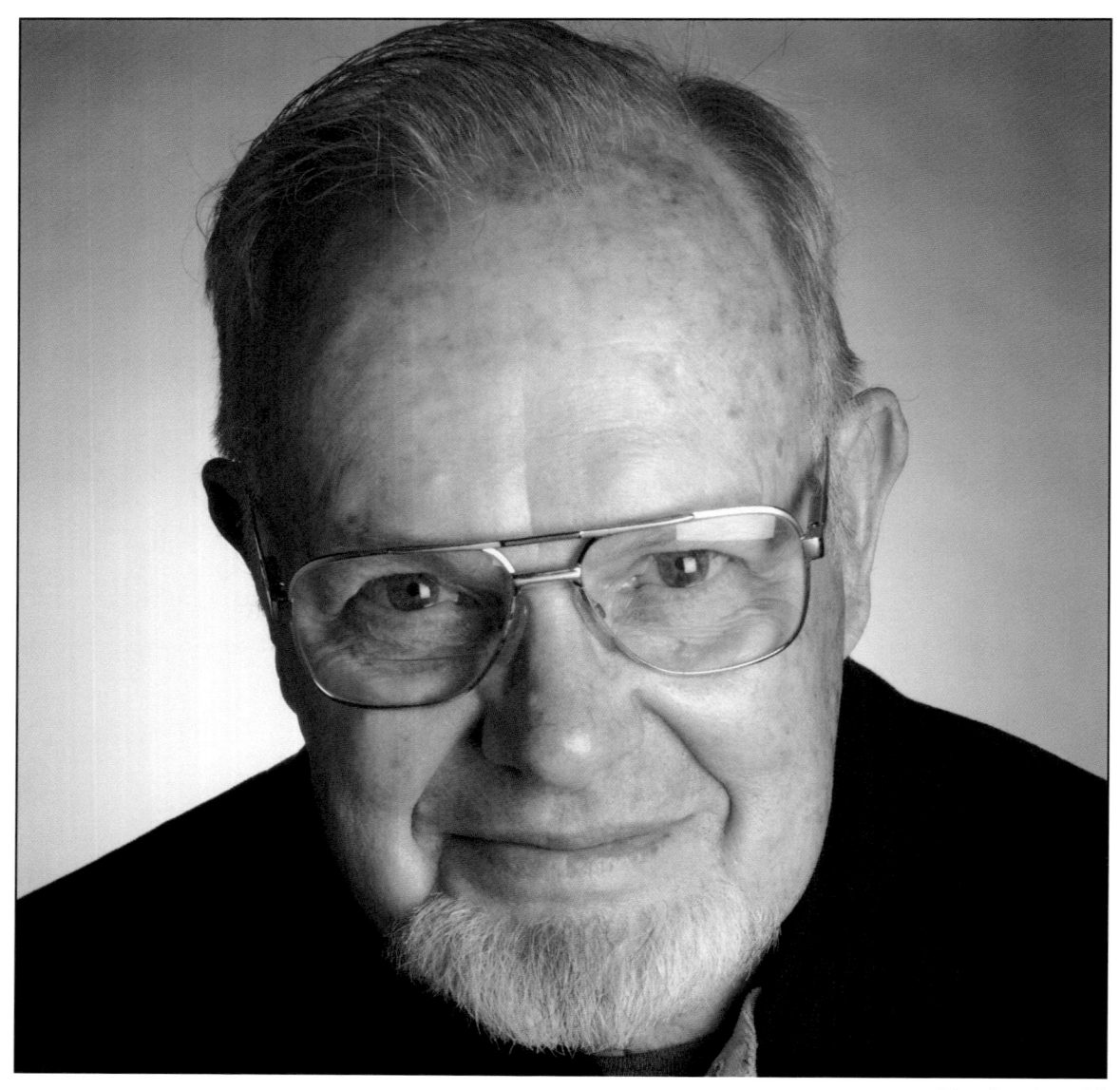

Charles Arnold

stilled for a moment

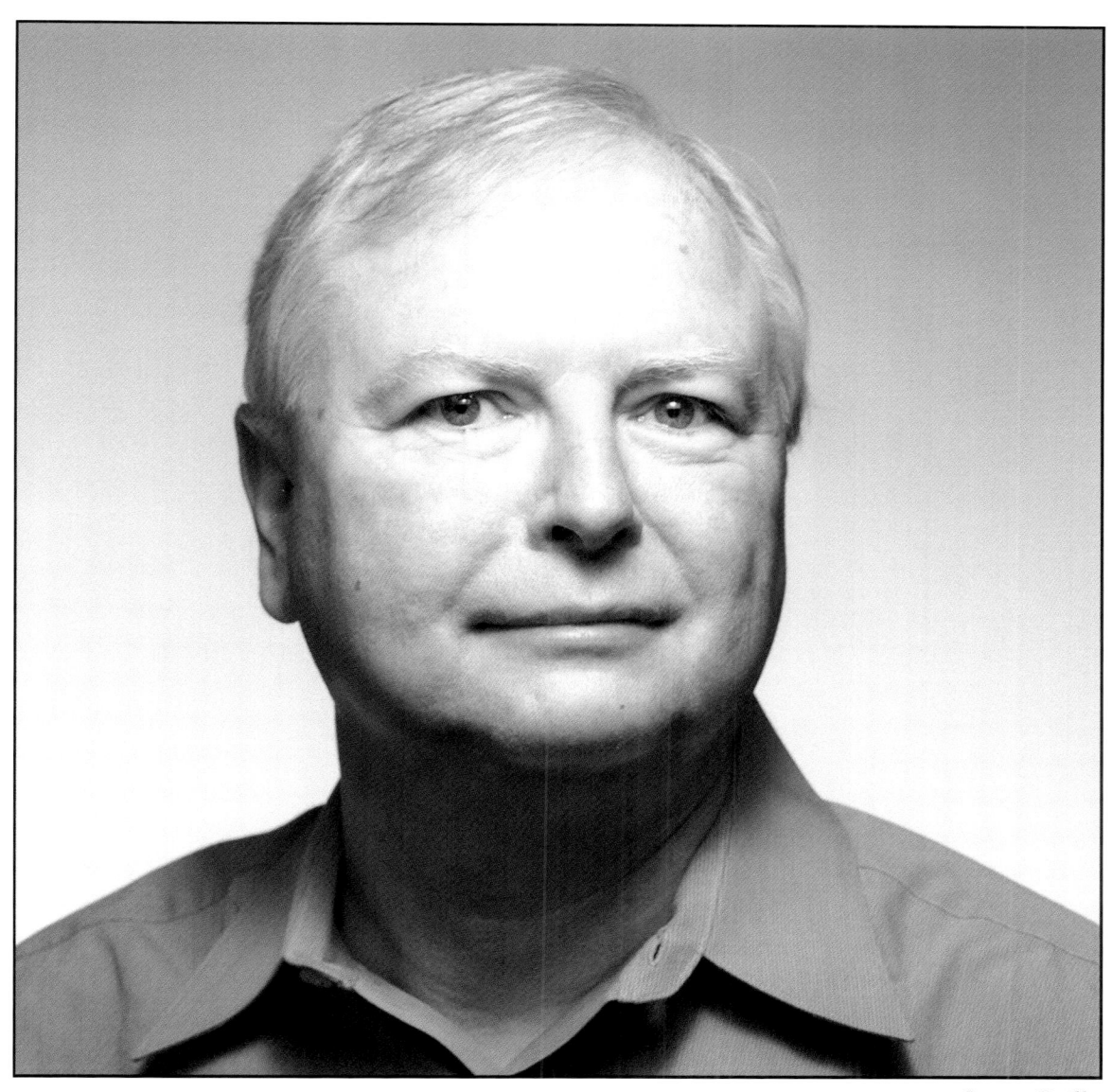

James Reilly

their chatter suspended

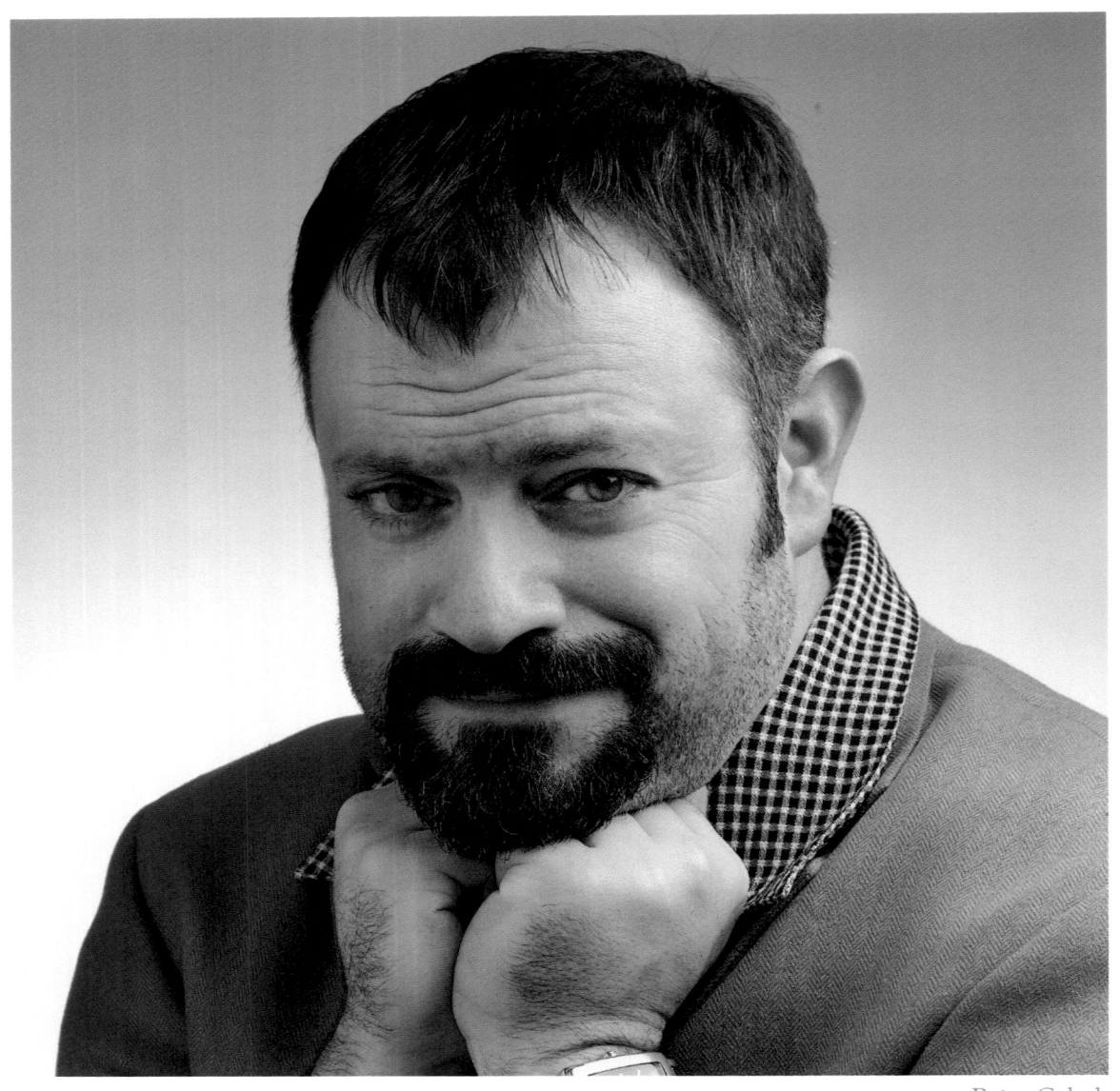

Peter Gabak

joy and grief contained.

Lindsay Cade

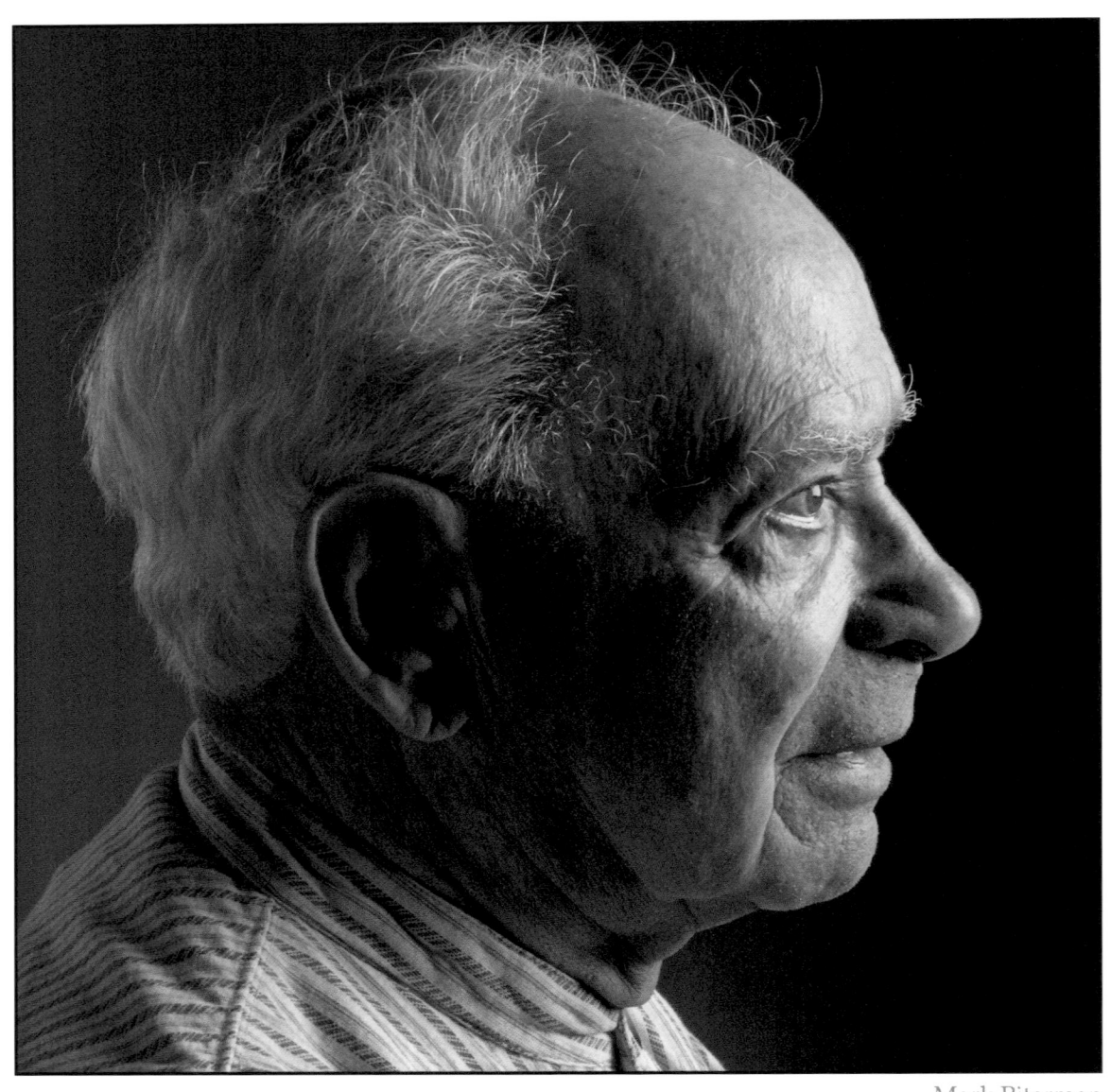

Mark Piterman

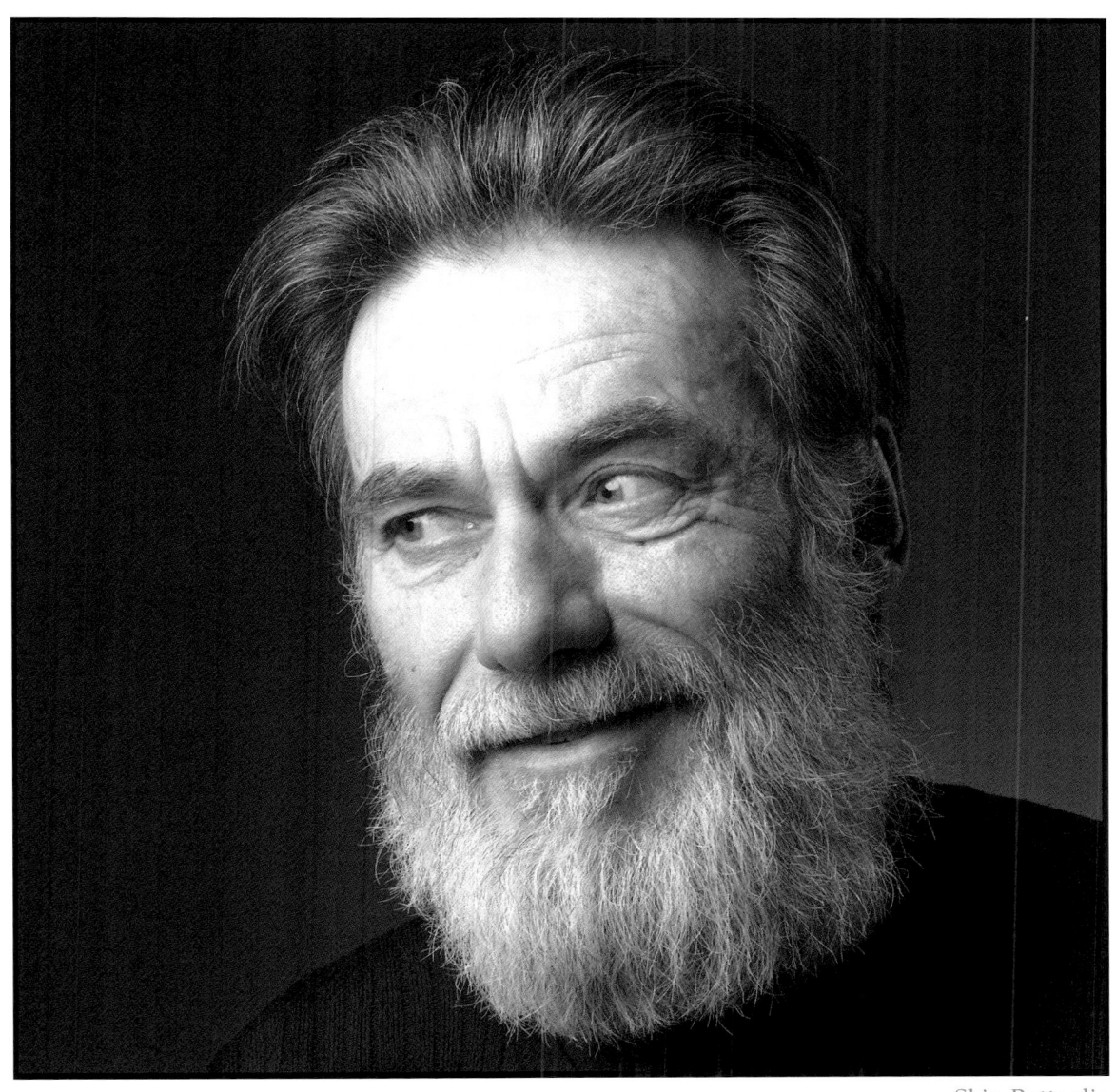

Skip Battaglia

Consider the light on the brow

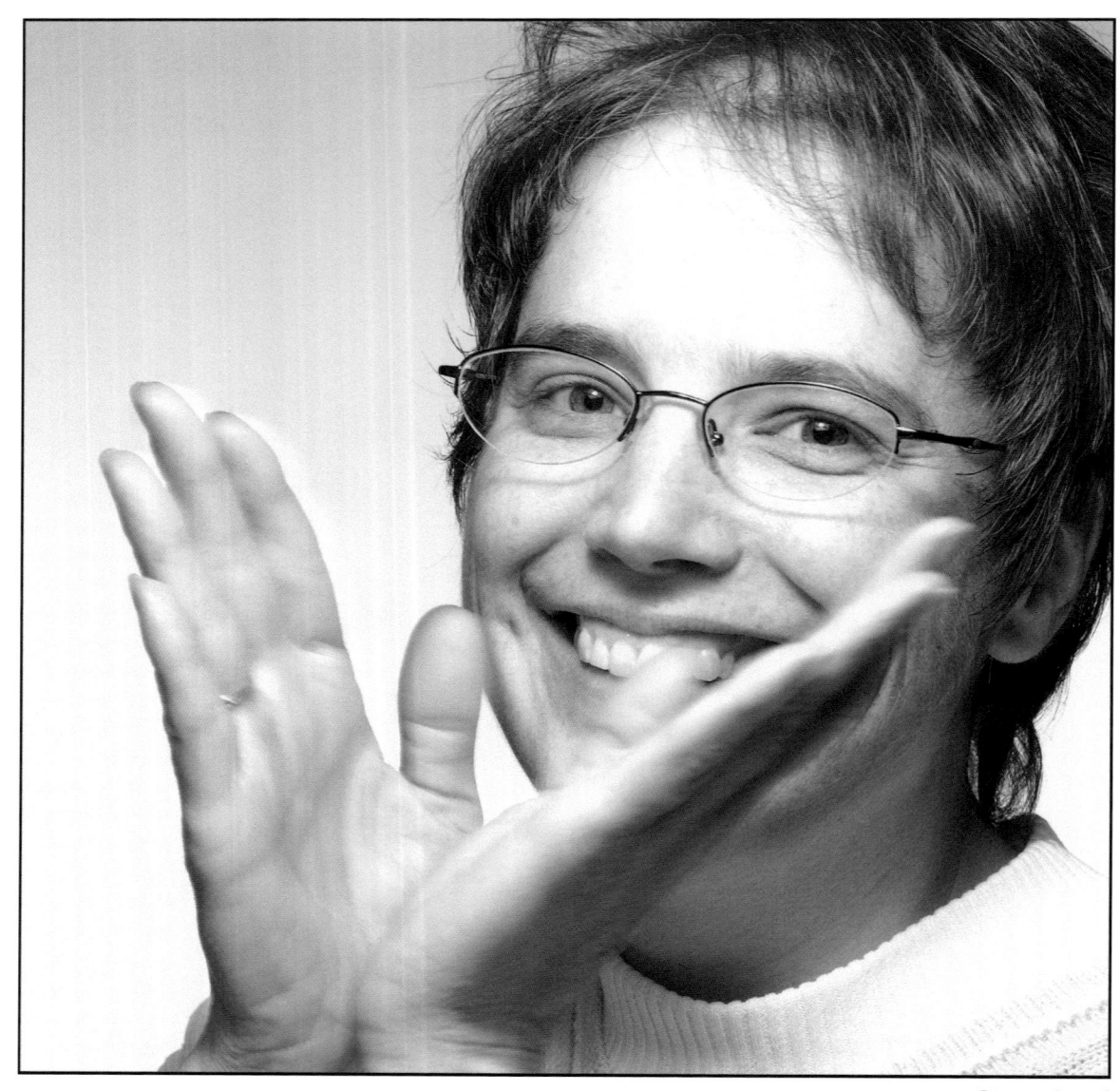

Ginny Orzel

light springing from hands

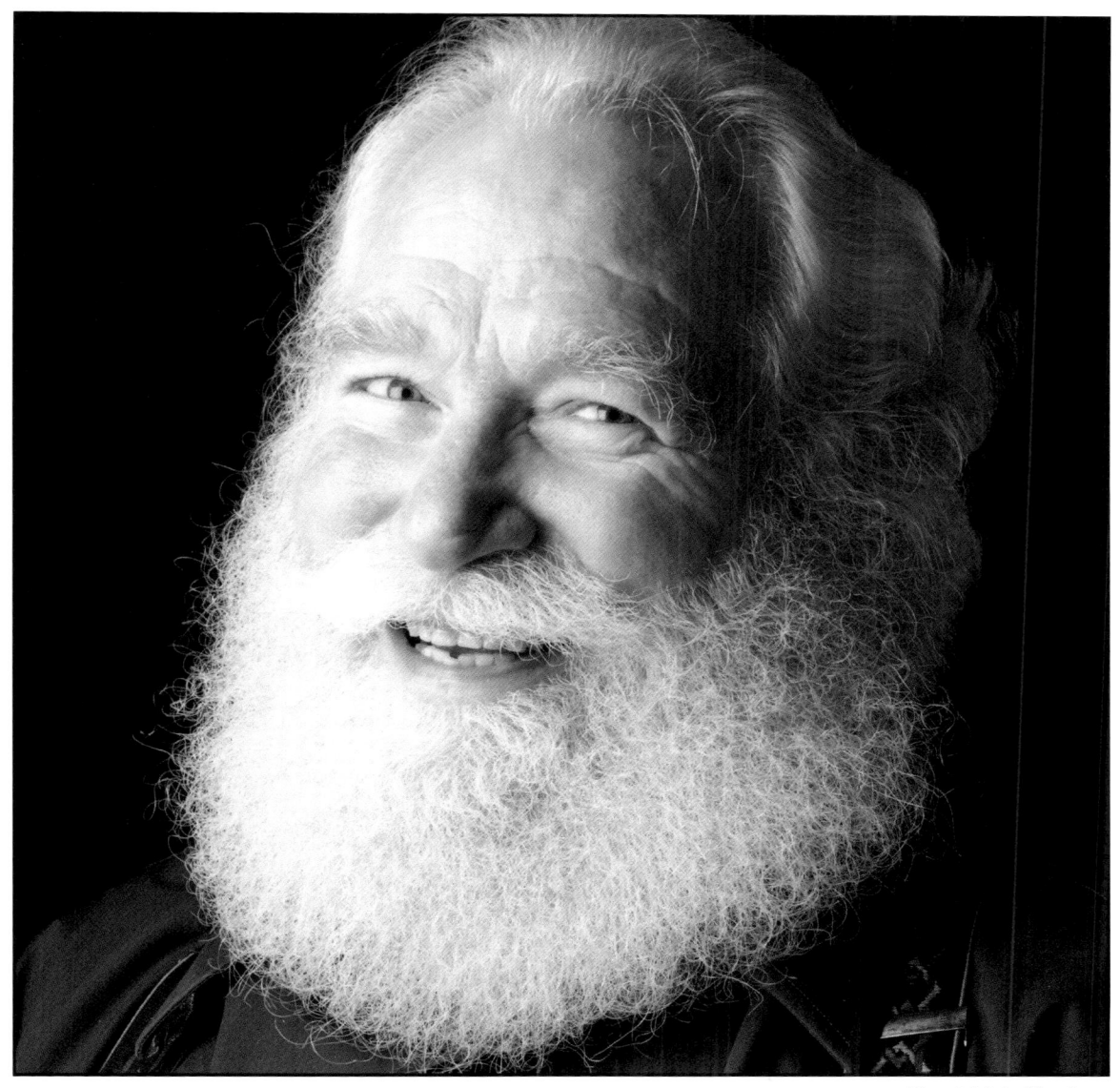

David McCloskey

hiding in a nest of beard

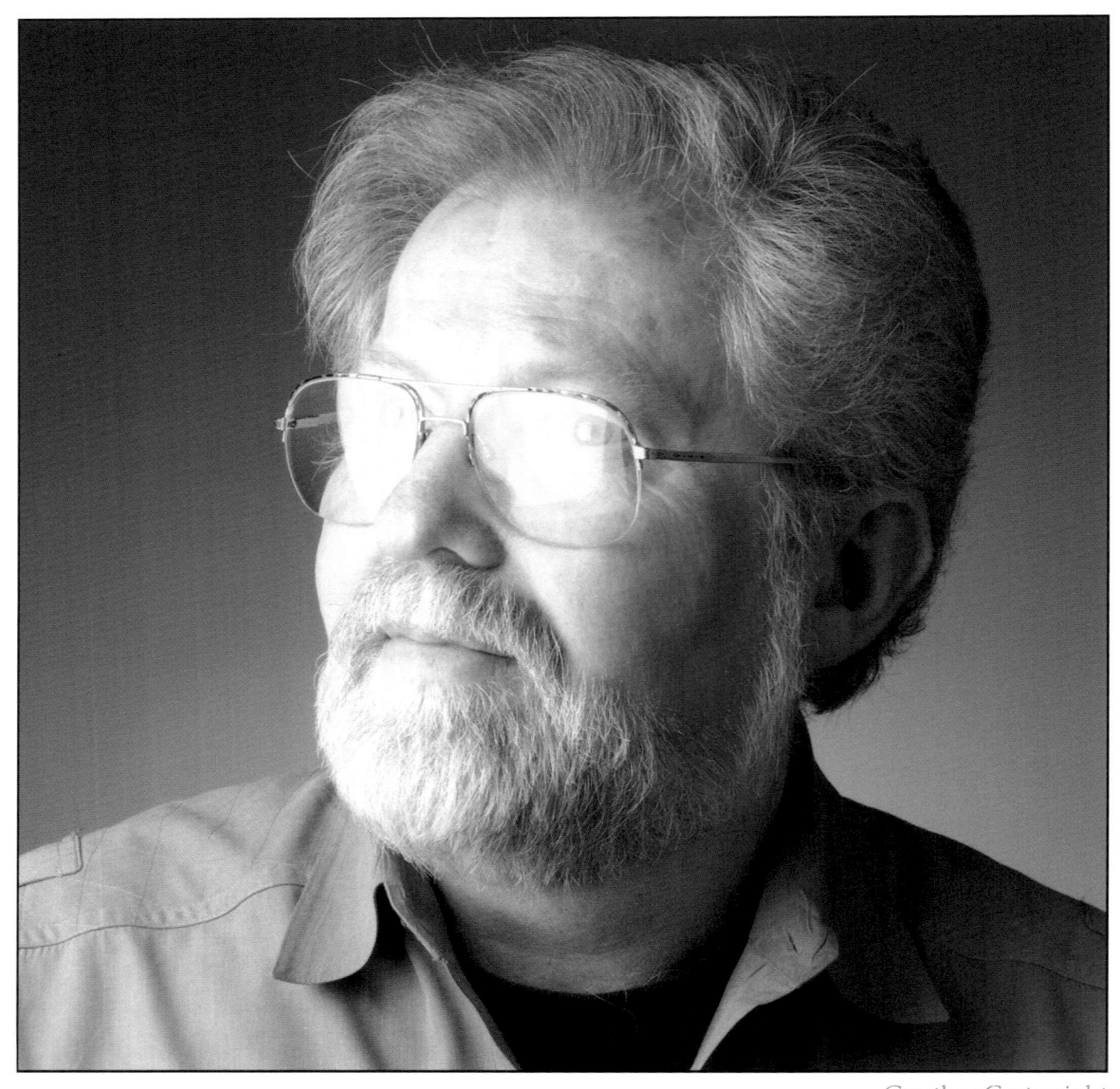

light palpable as paint

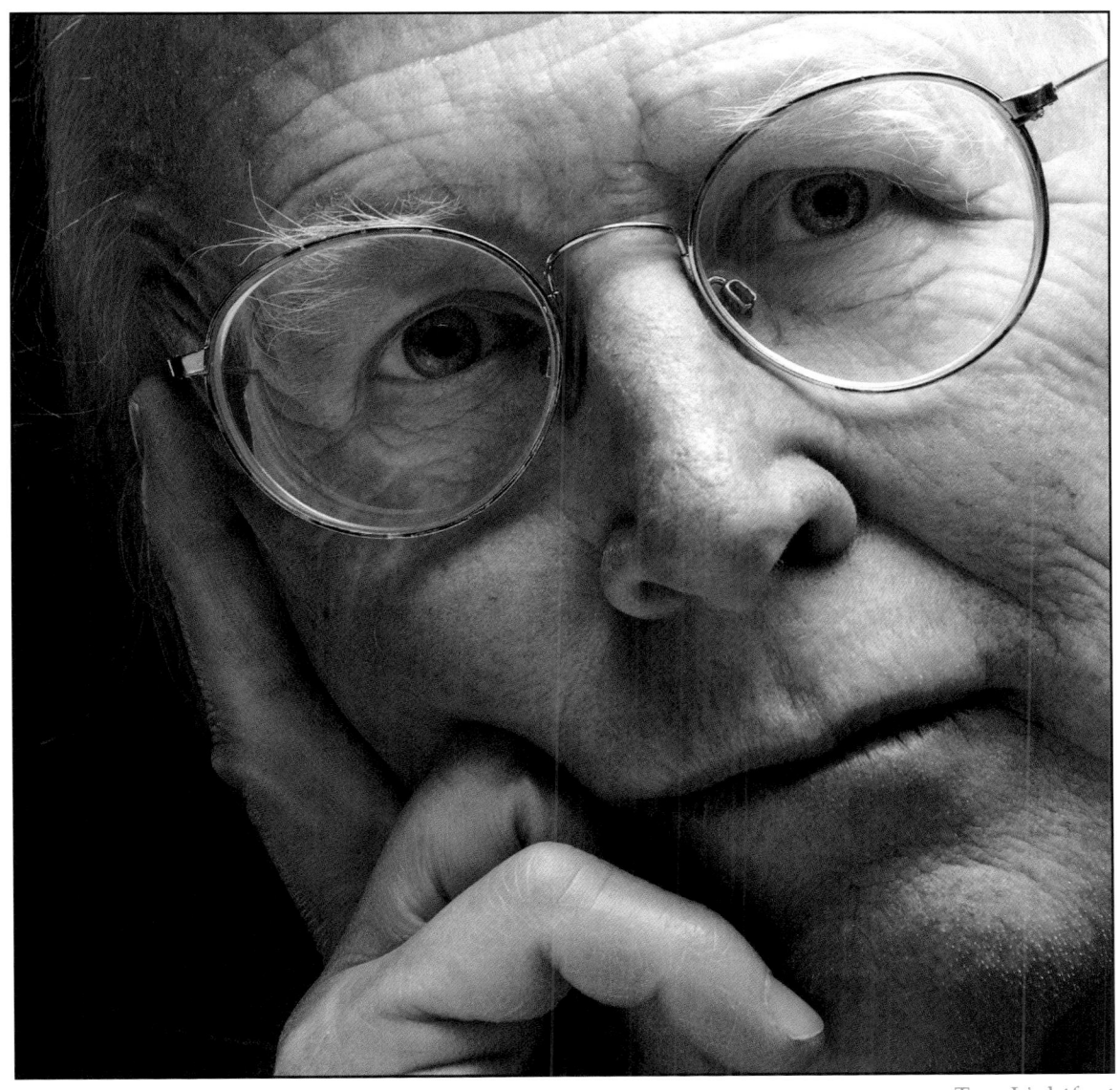

Tom Lightfoot

fragile as glass.

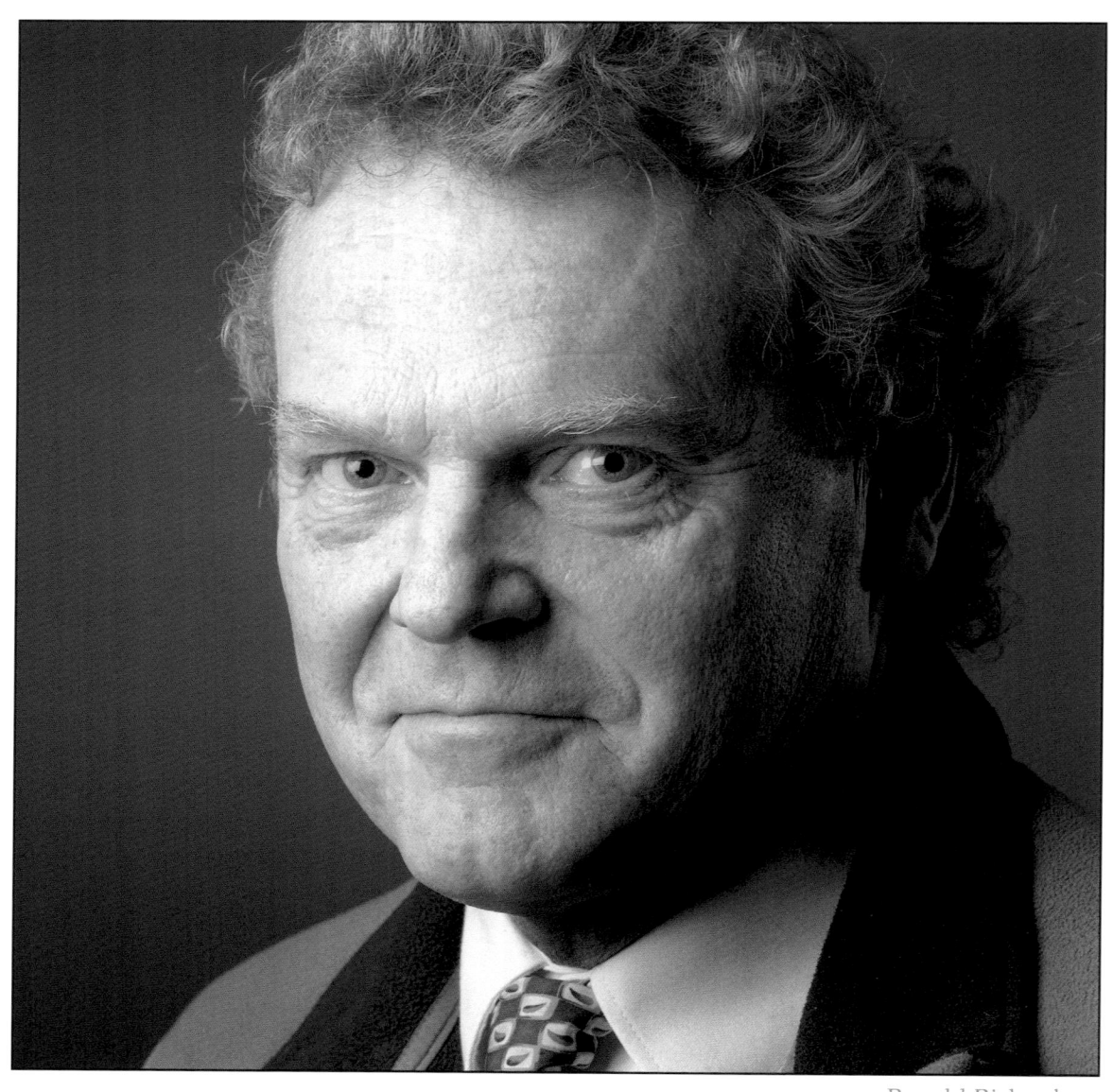

Ronald Richardson

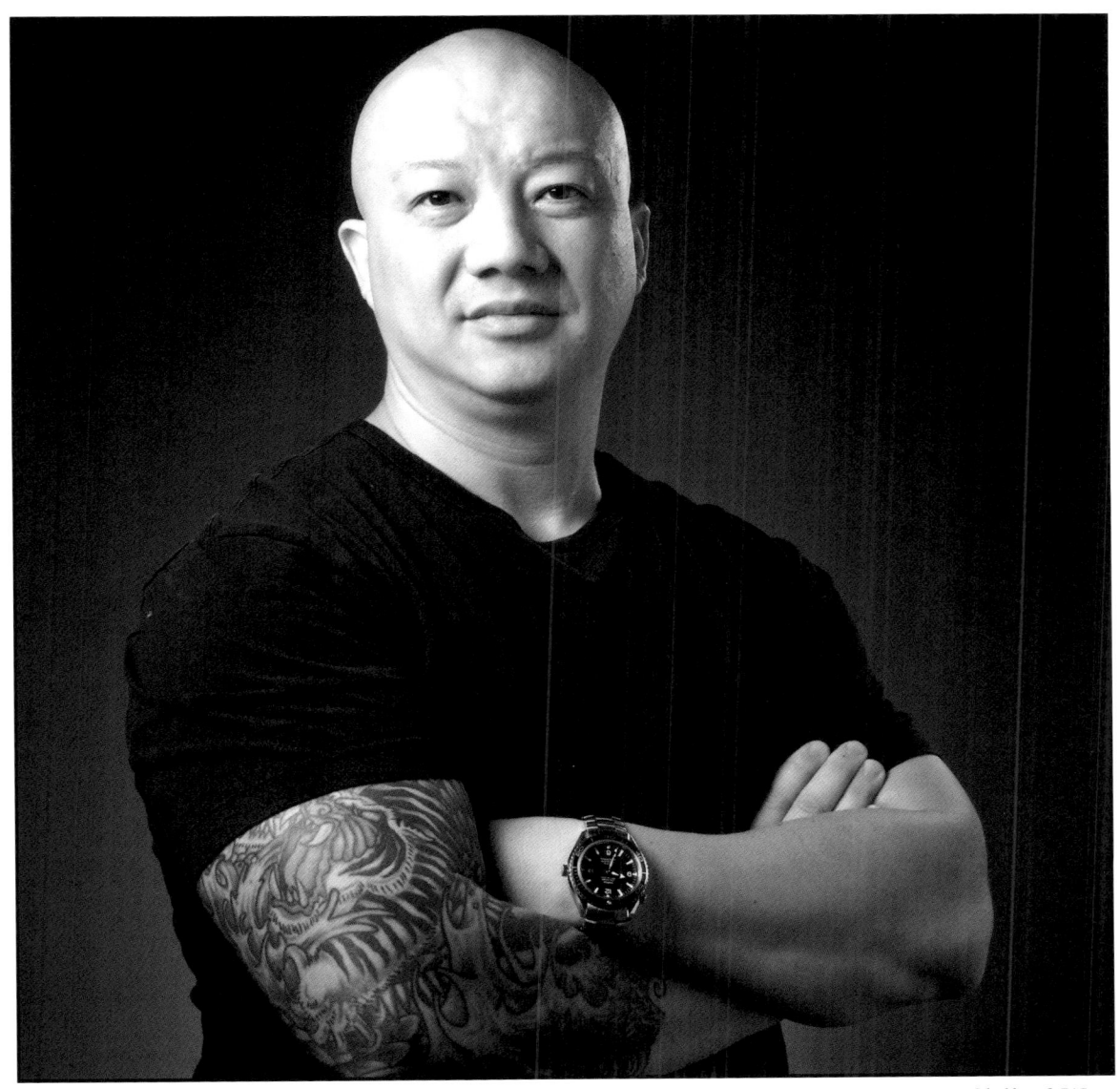

Clifford Wun

Enter the eyes

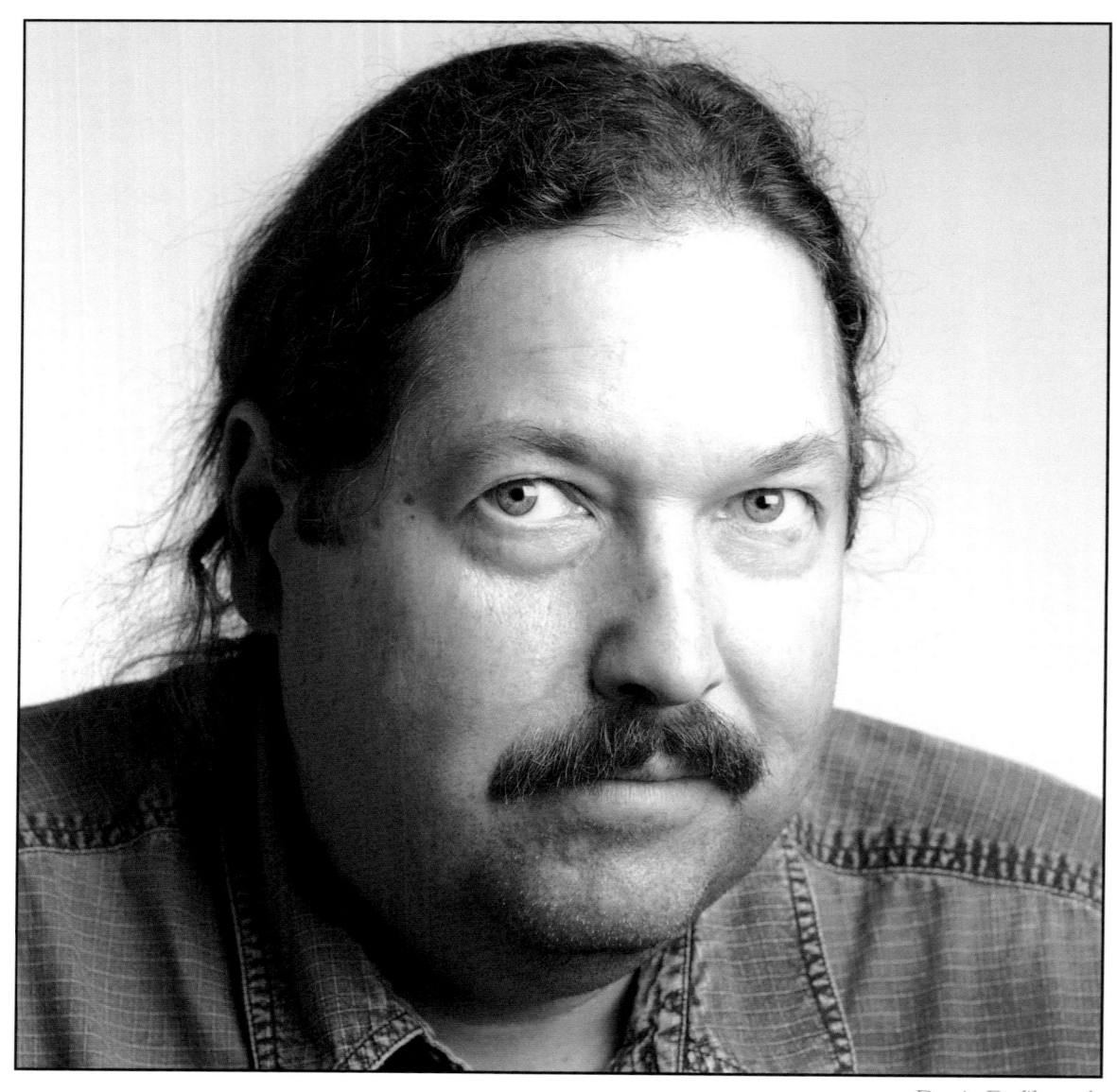

Denis Defibaugh

as professor becomes sitter

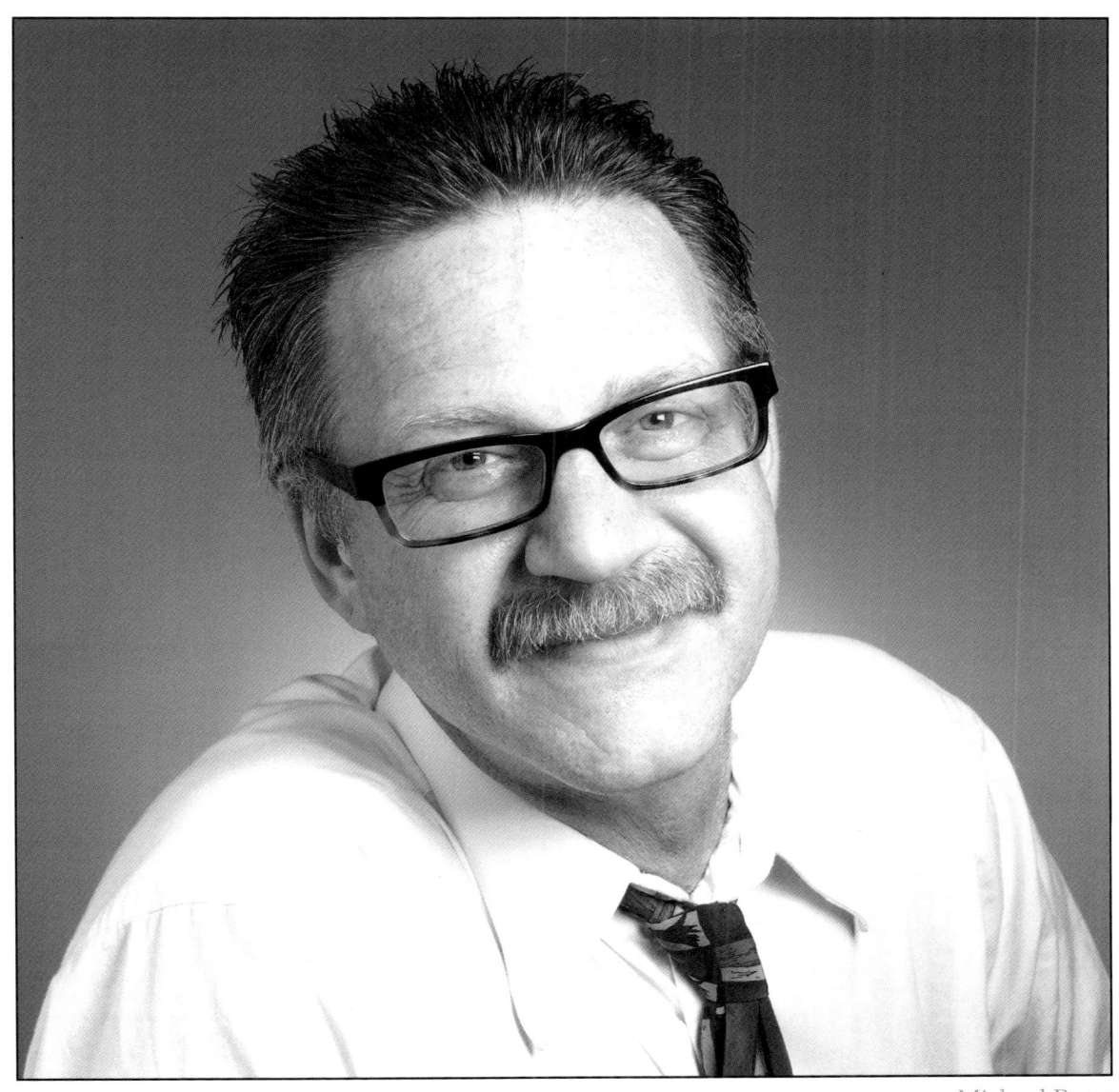

Michael Peres

becomes subject

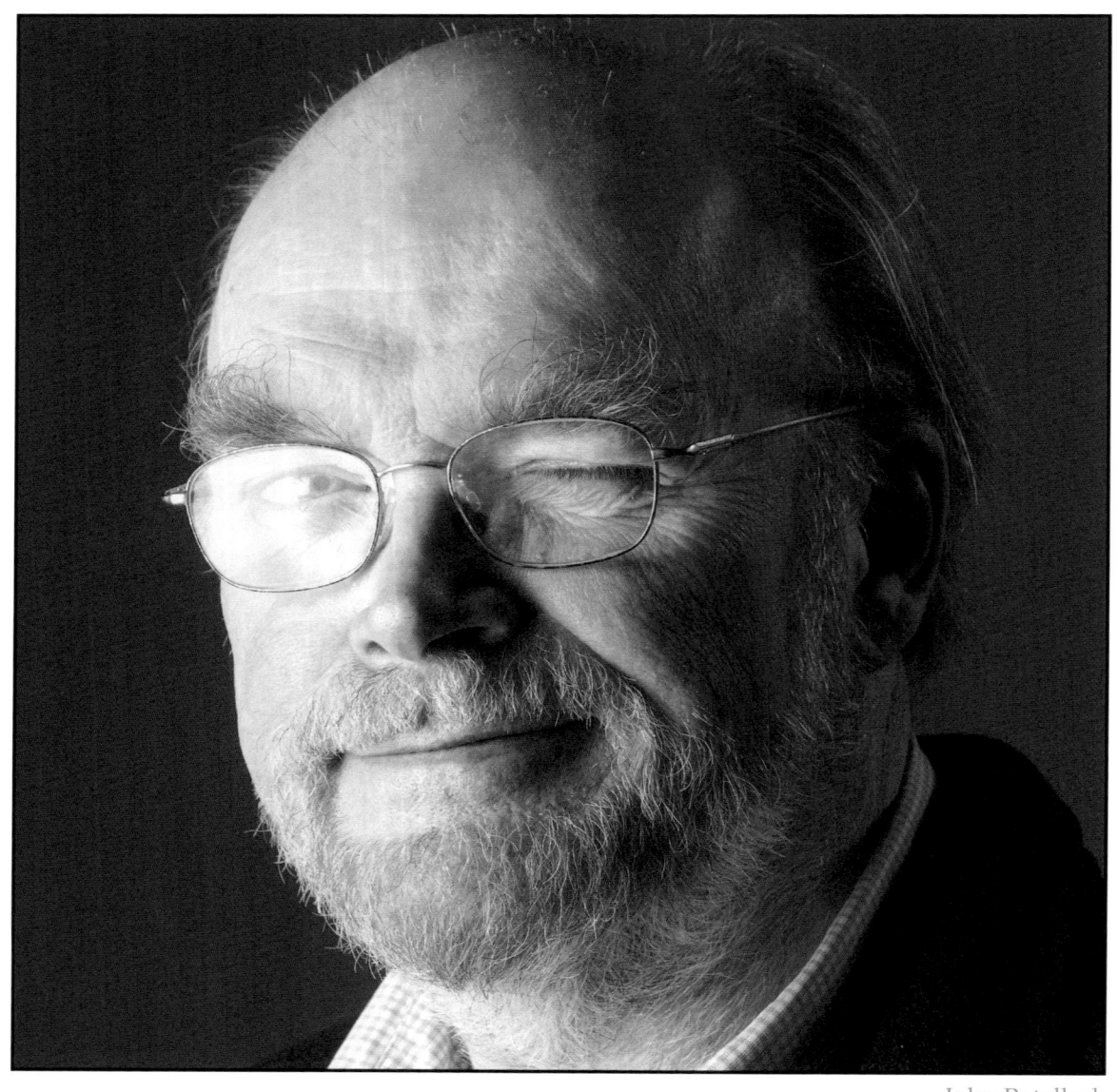

hair, whiskers, and spectacles

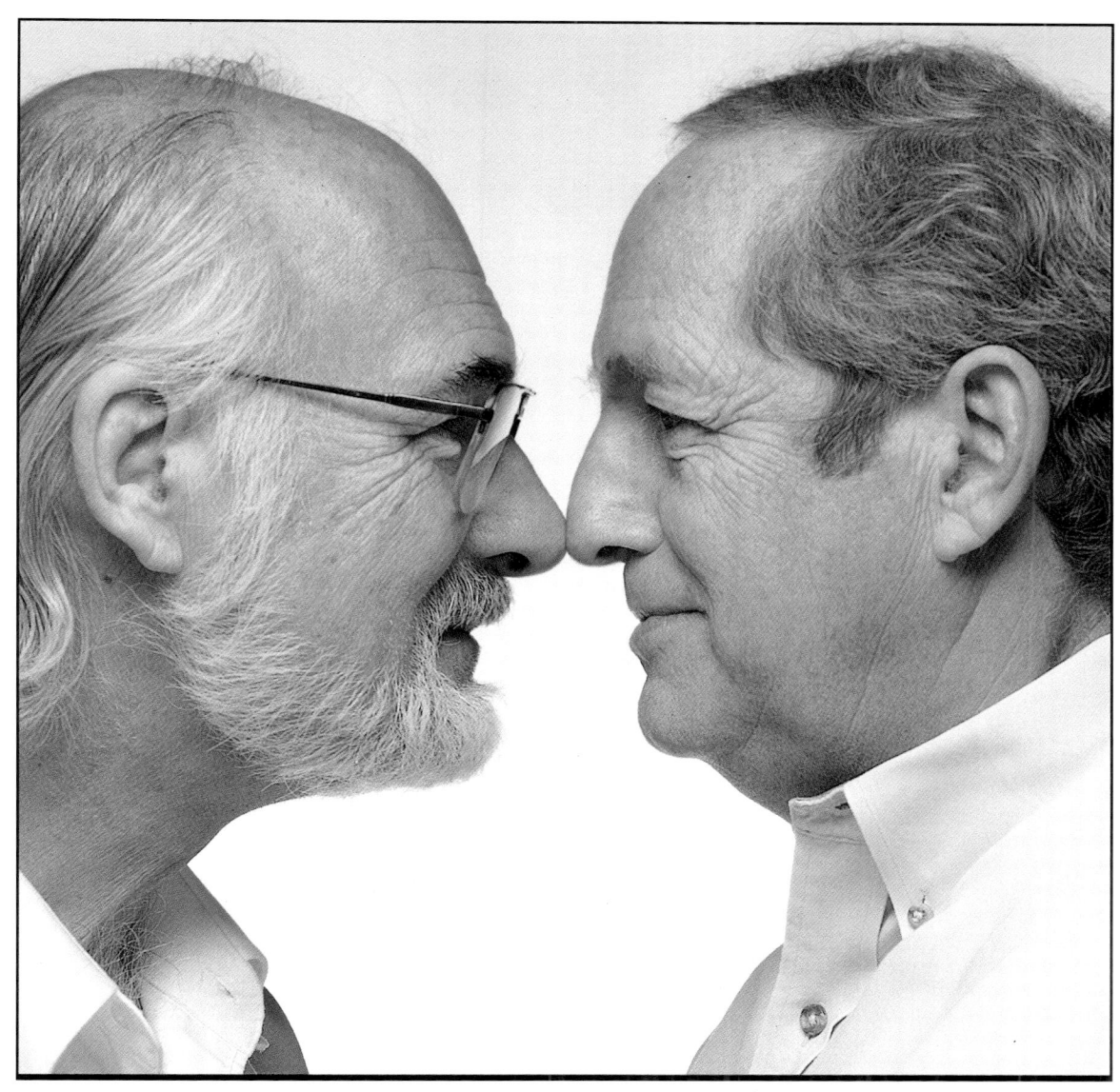

Andrew Davidhazy and Bill DuBois

gloriously scrutinized;

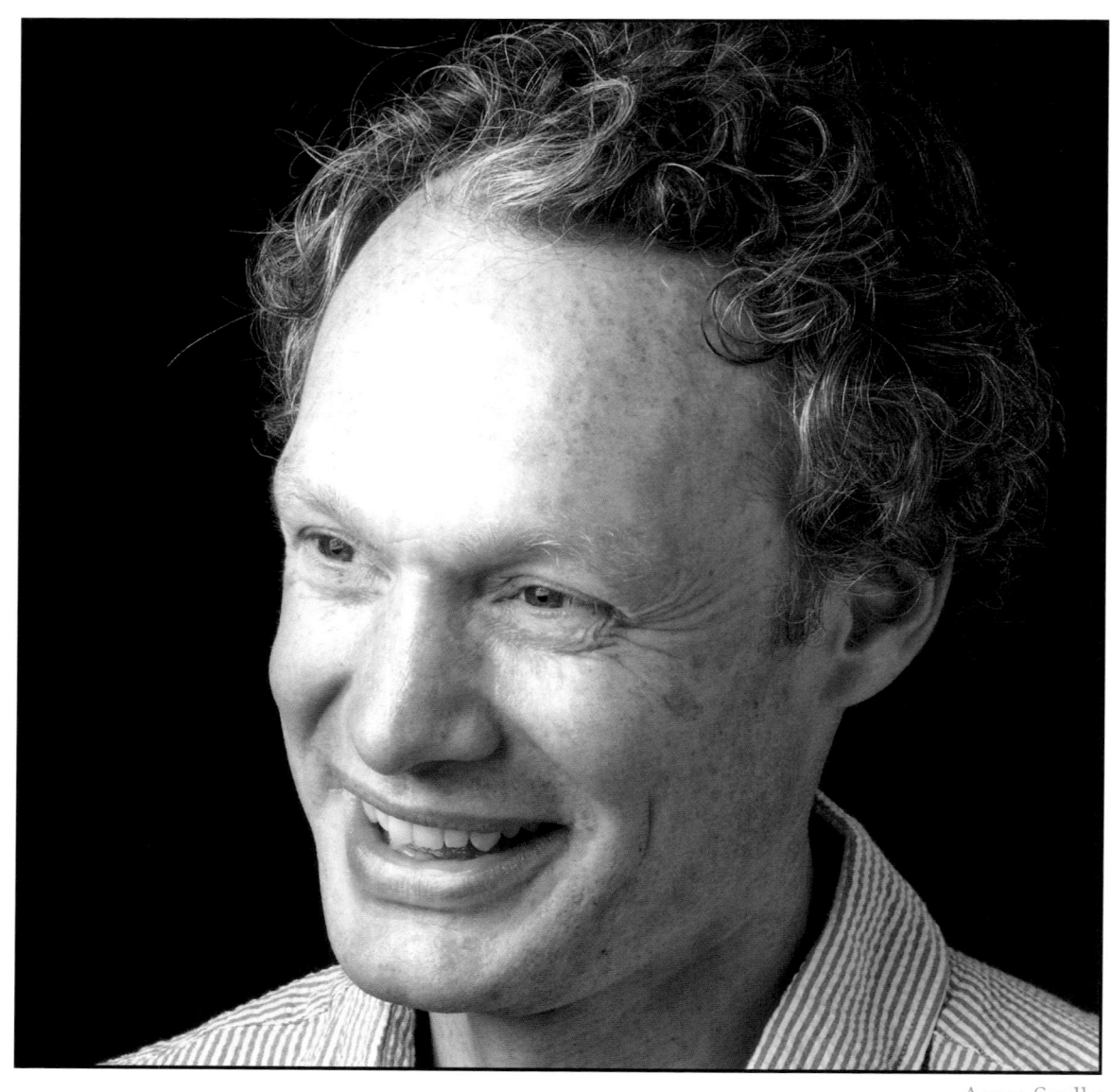

Amos Scully

wrinkles a landscape

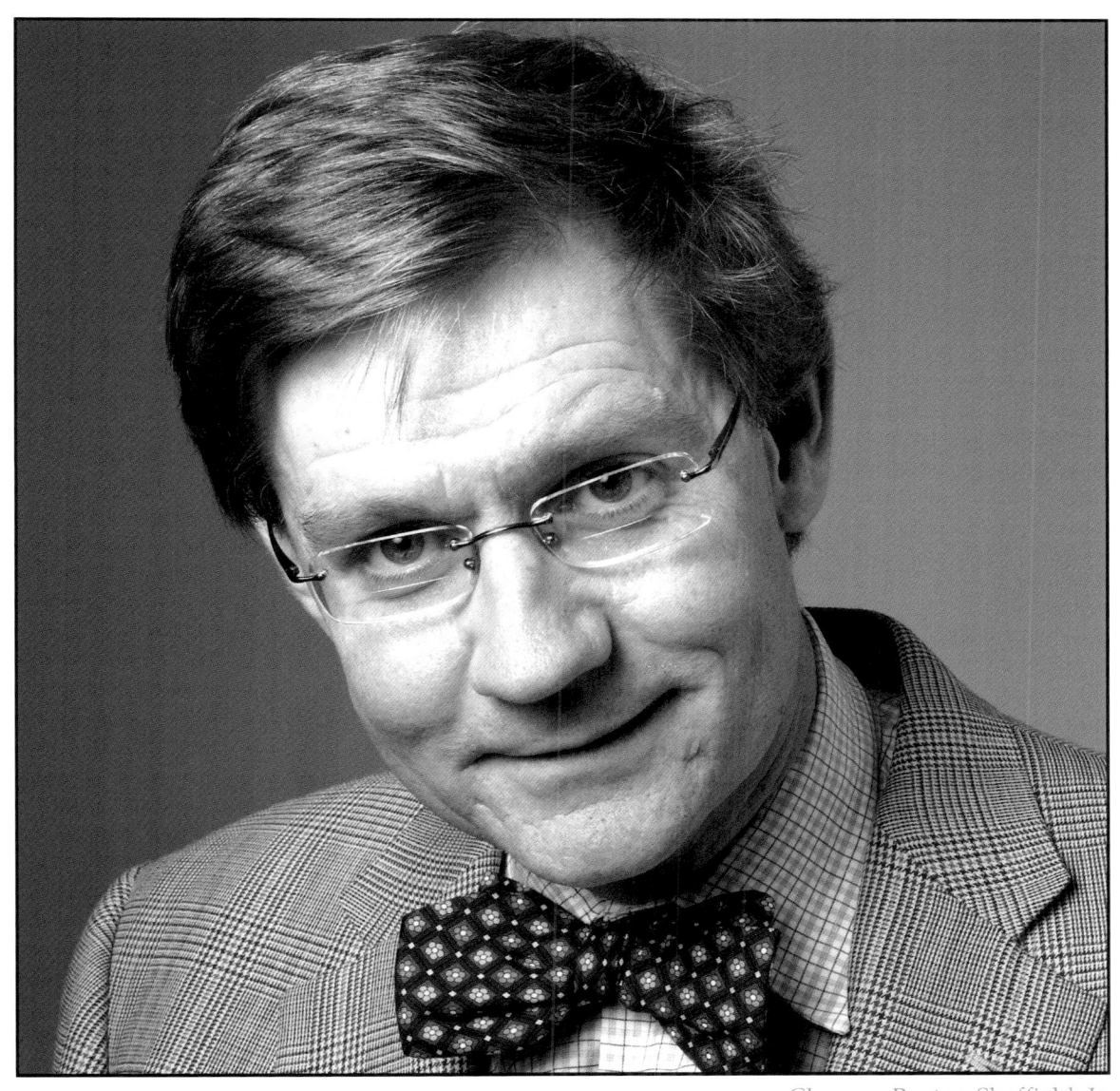

Clarence Burton Sheffield, Jr.

shaped by the tide.

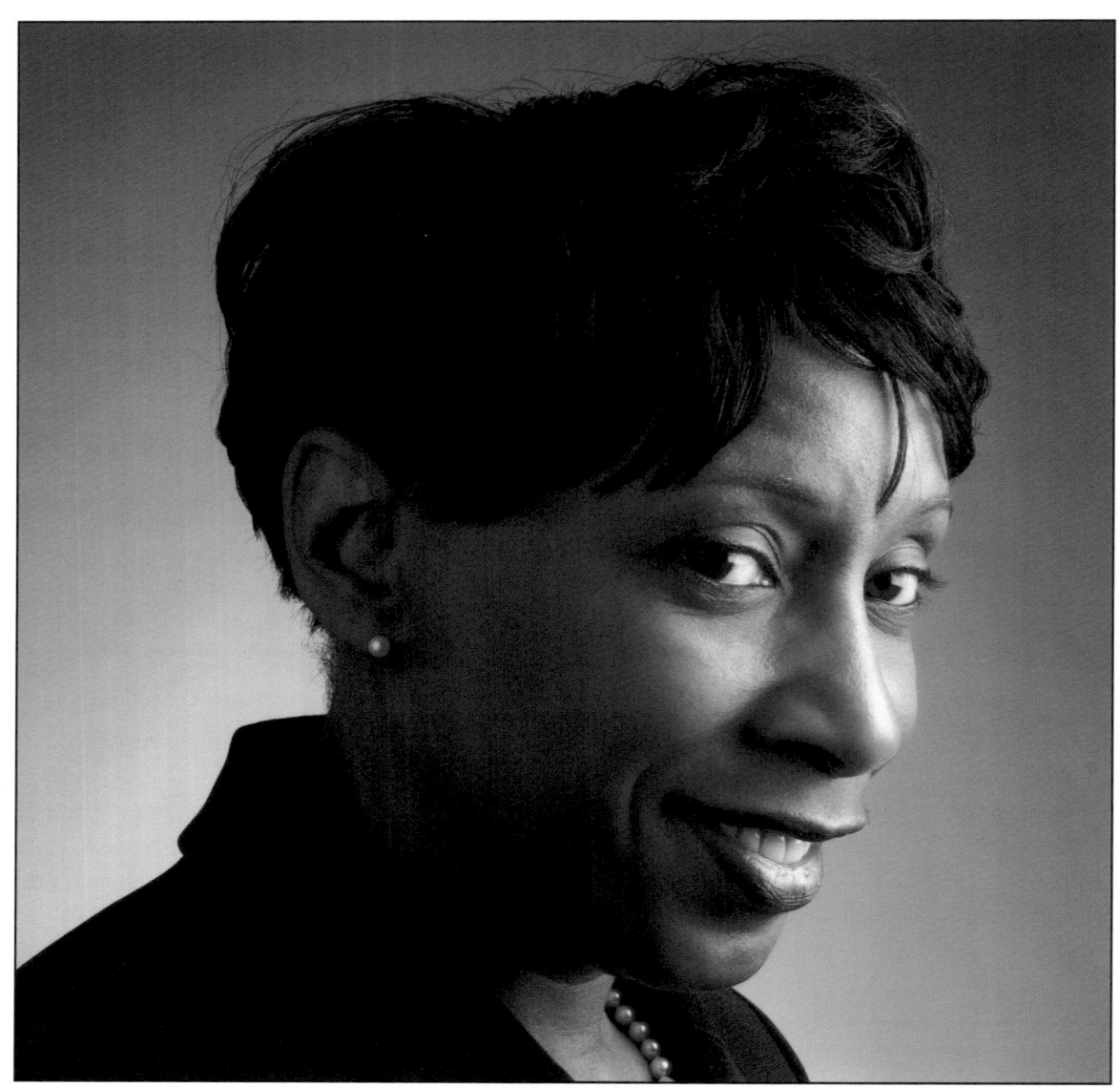

Alfreda Brown

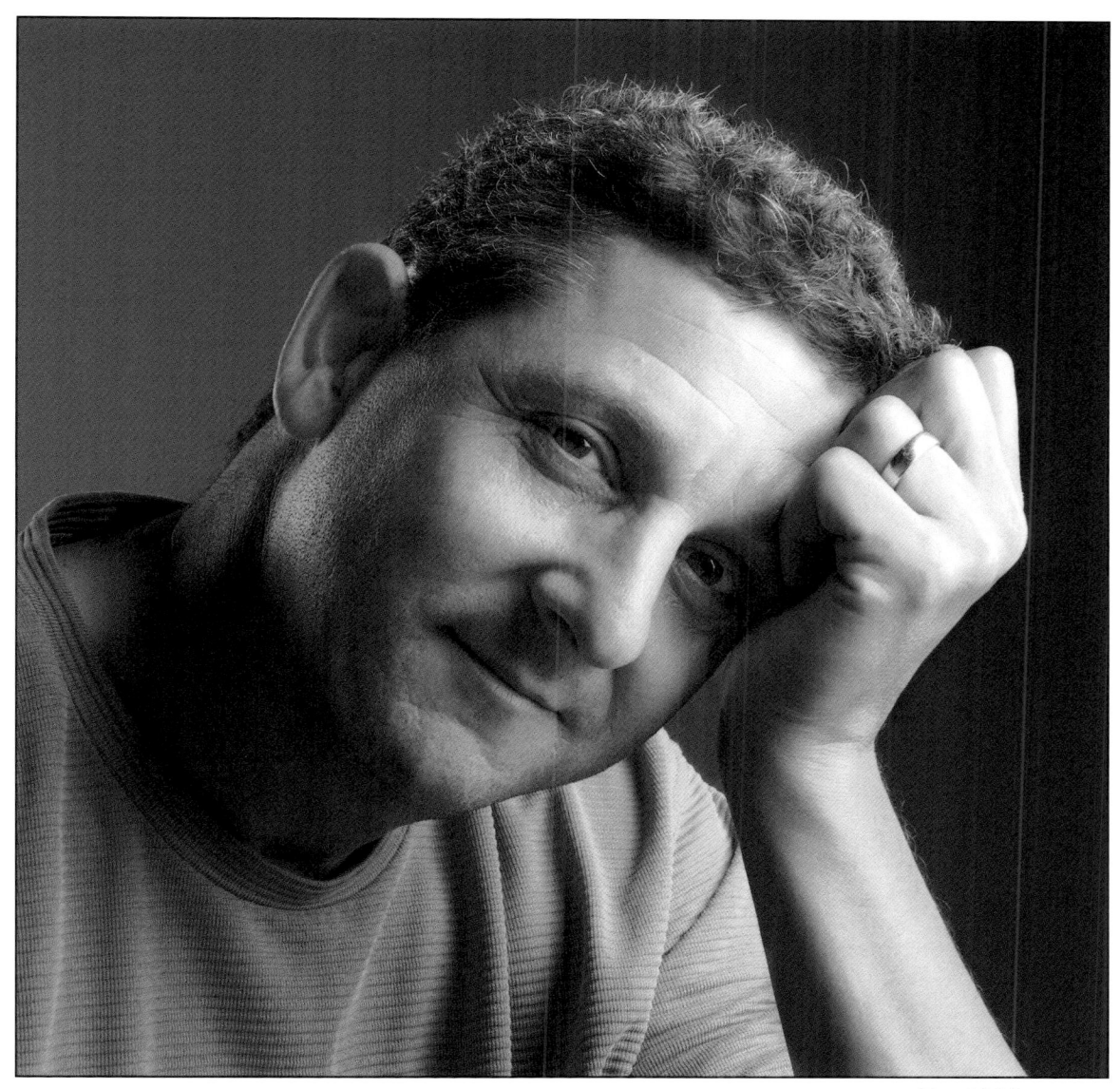

David Neumann

Watch for the hands

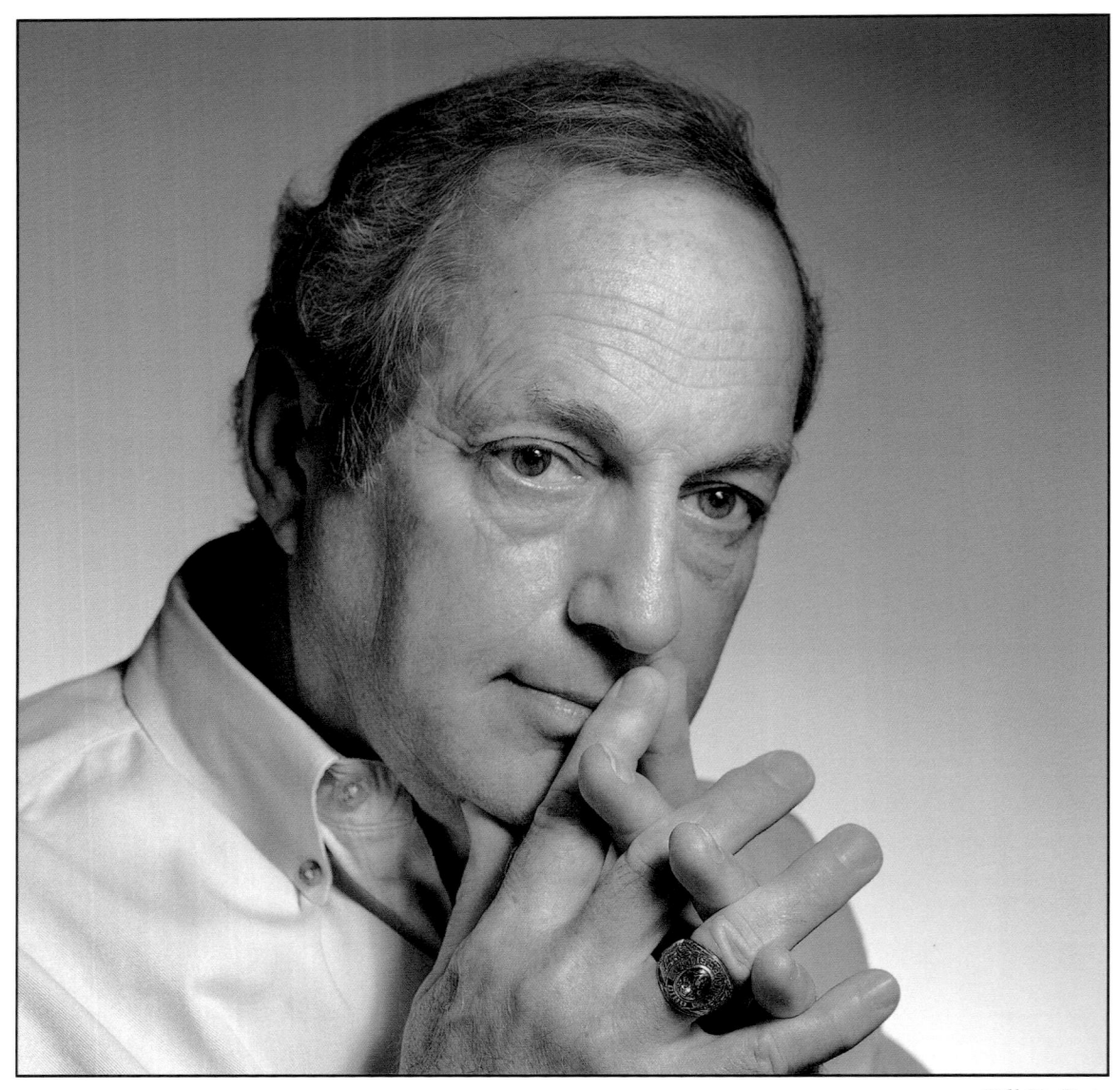

Bill DuBois

folded, ringed,

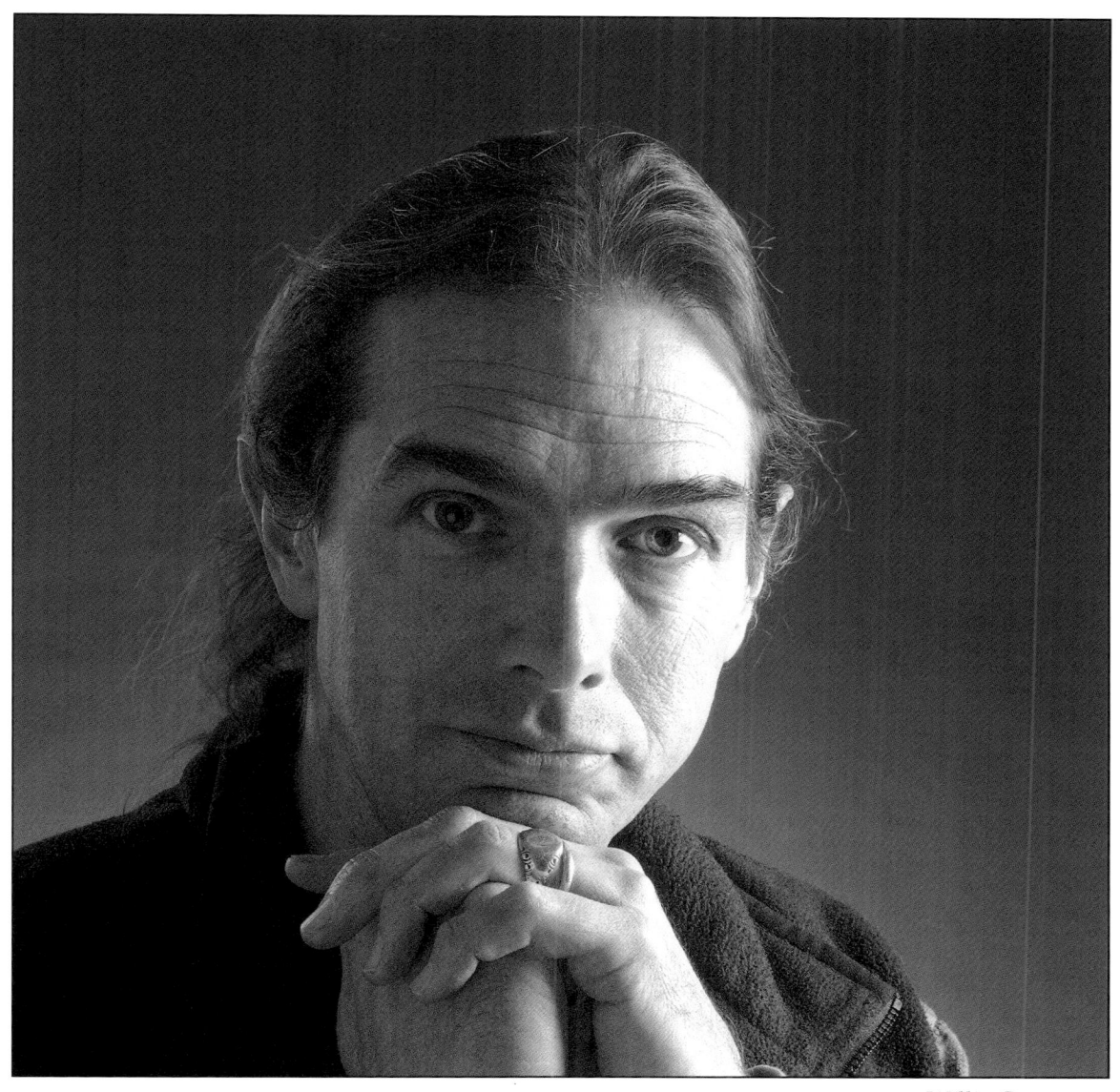

Willie Osterman

clenched to jaw, to elbow,

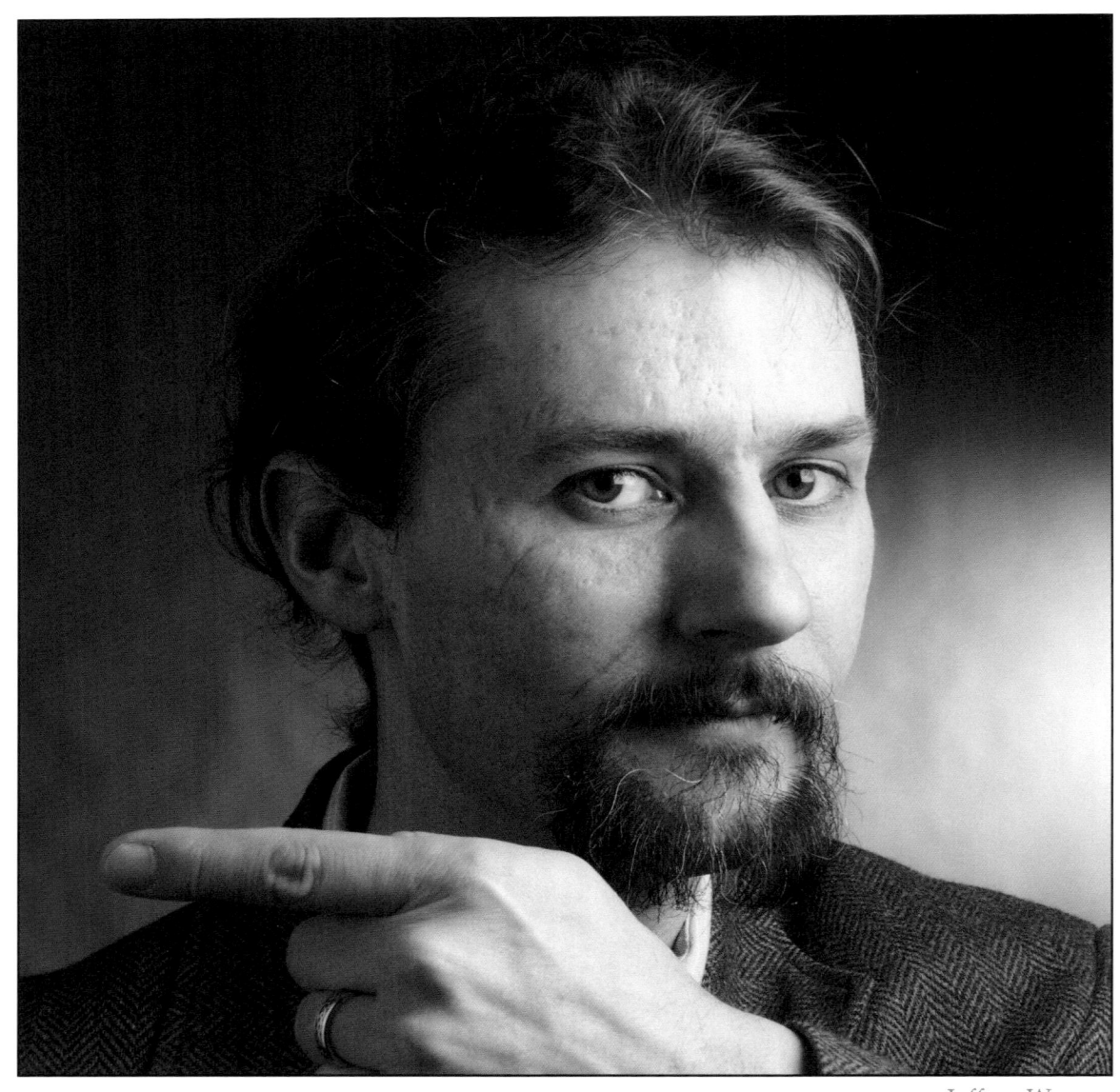

butterflied, pointing that-away

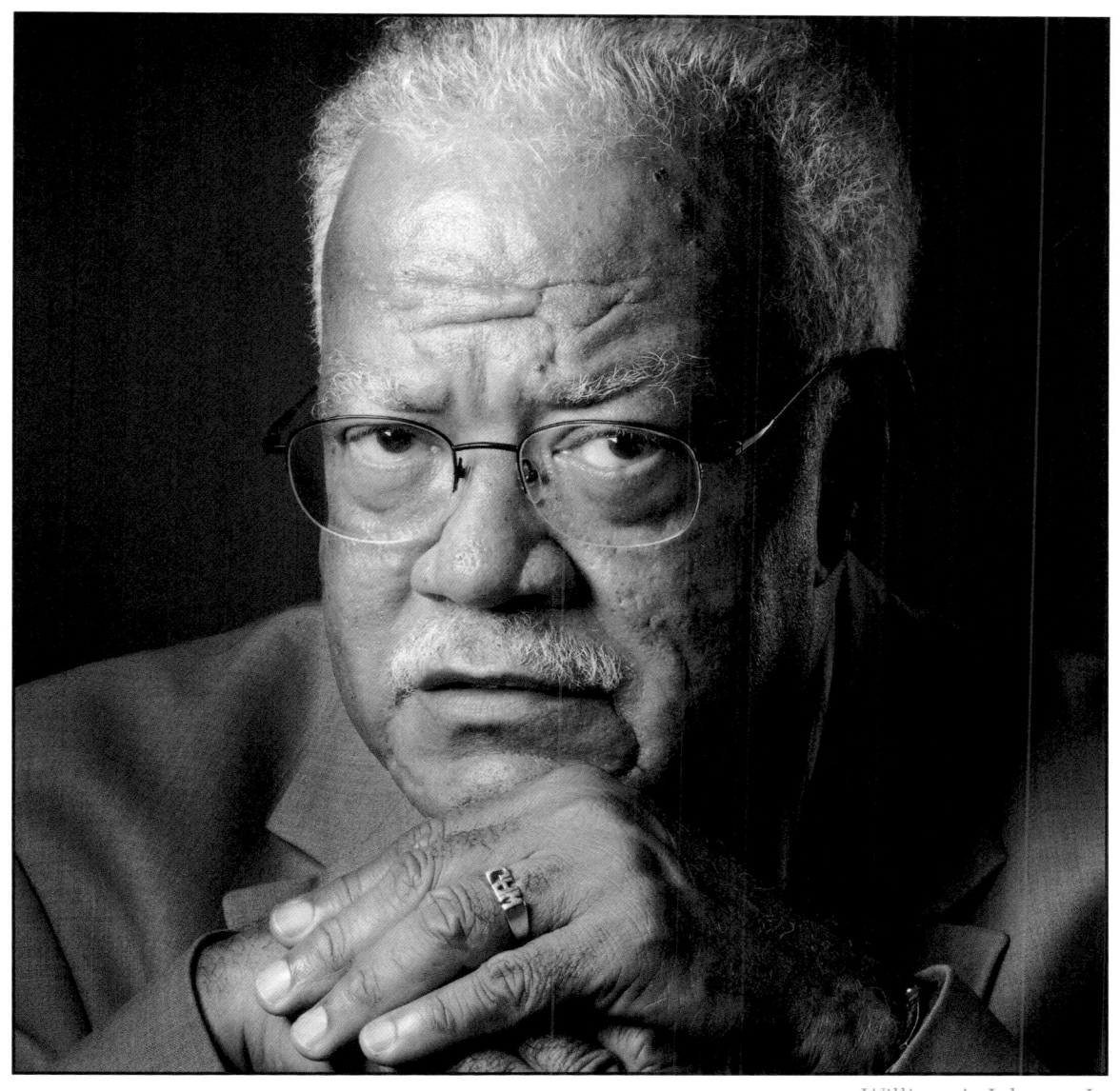

William A. Johnson Jr.

beyond the frame.

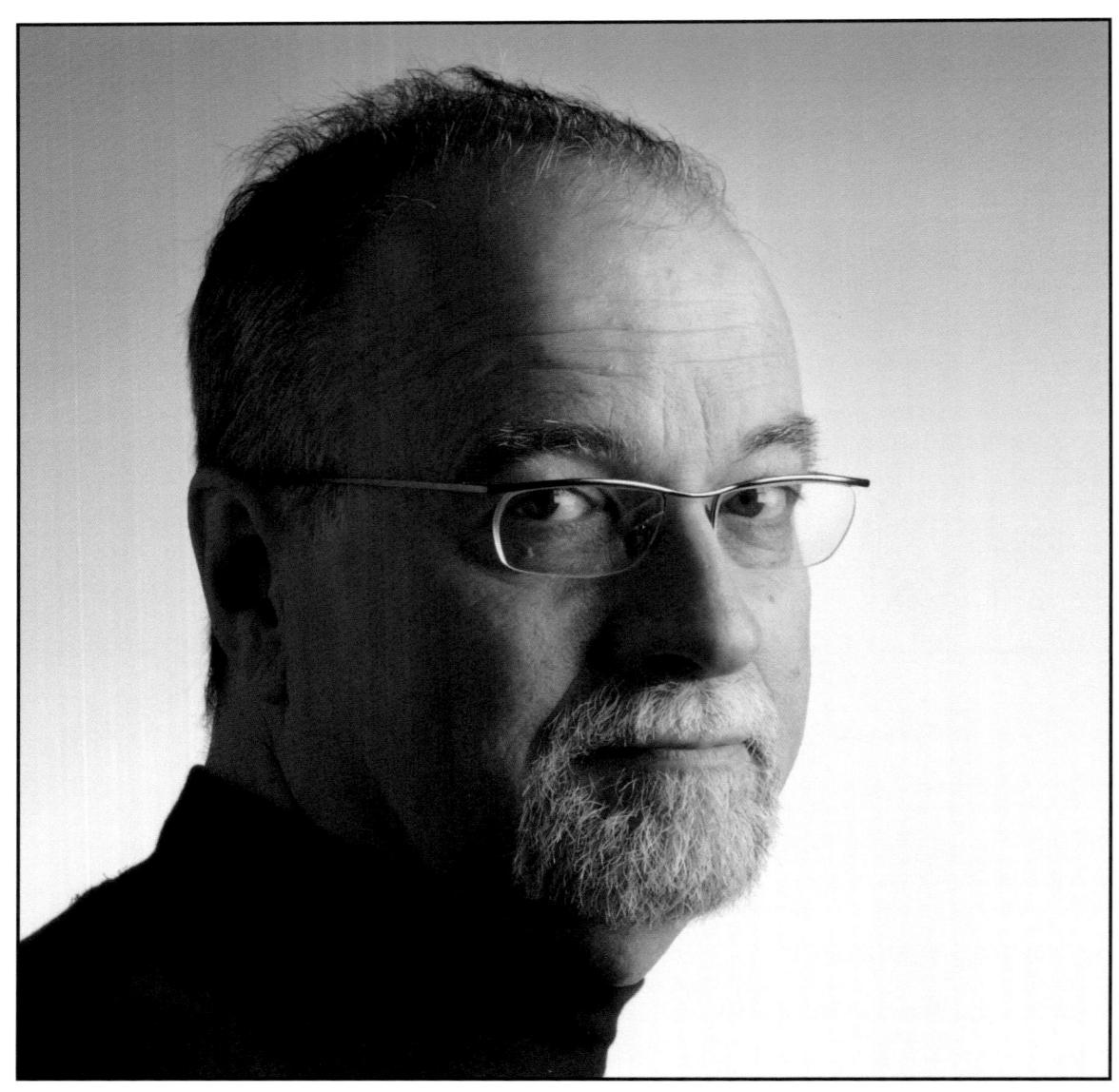

Doug Rea

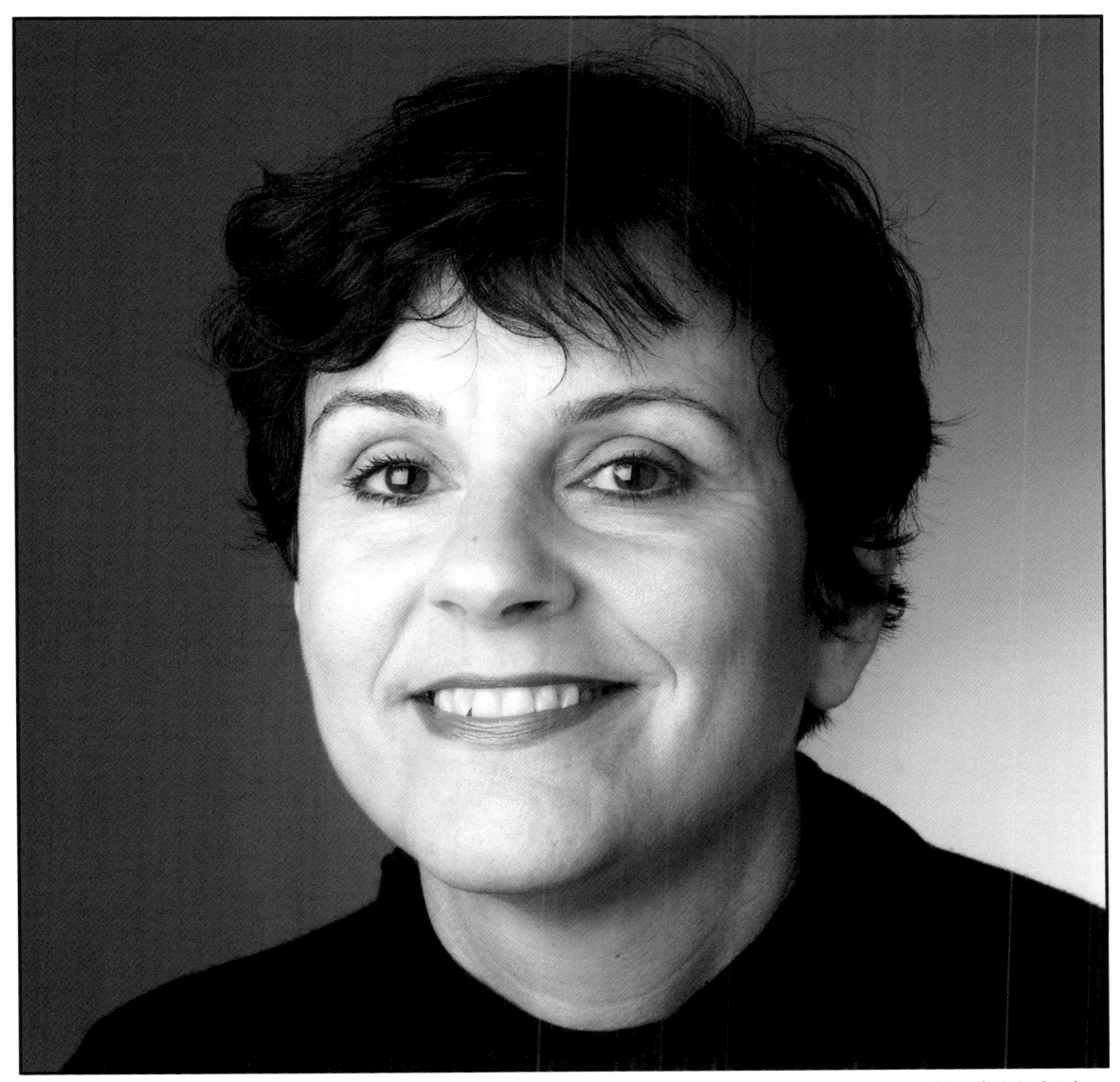

Heidi Nickisher

Enter the eyes

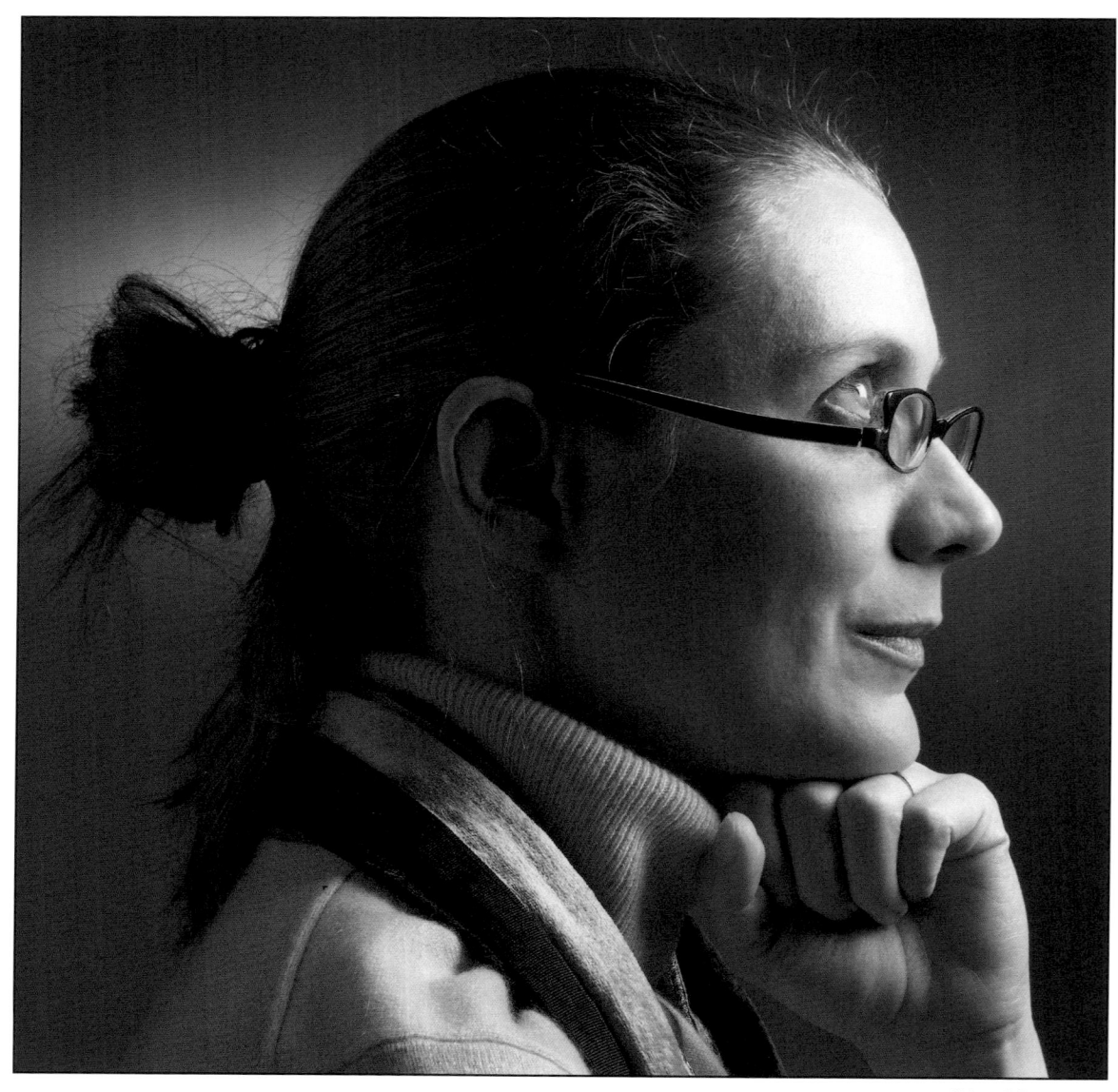

Lisa Hermsen

off center, winking, singular

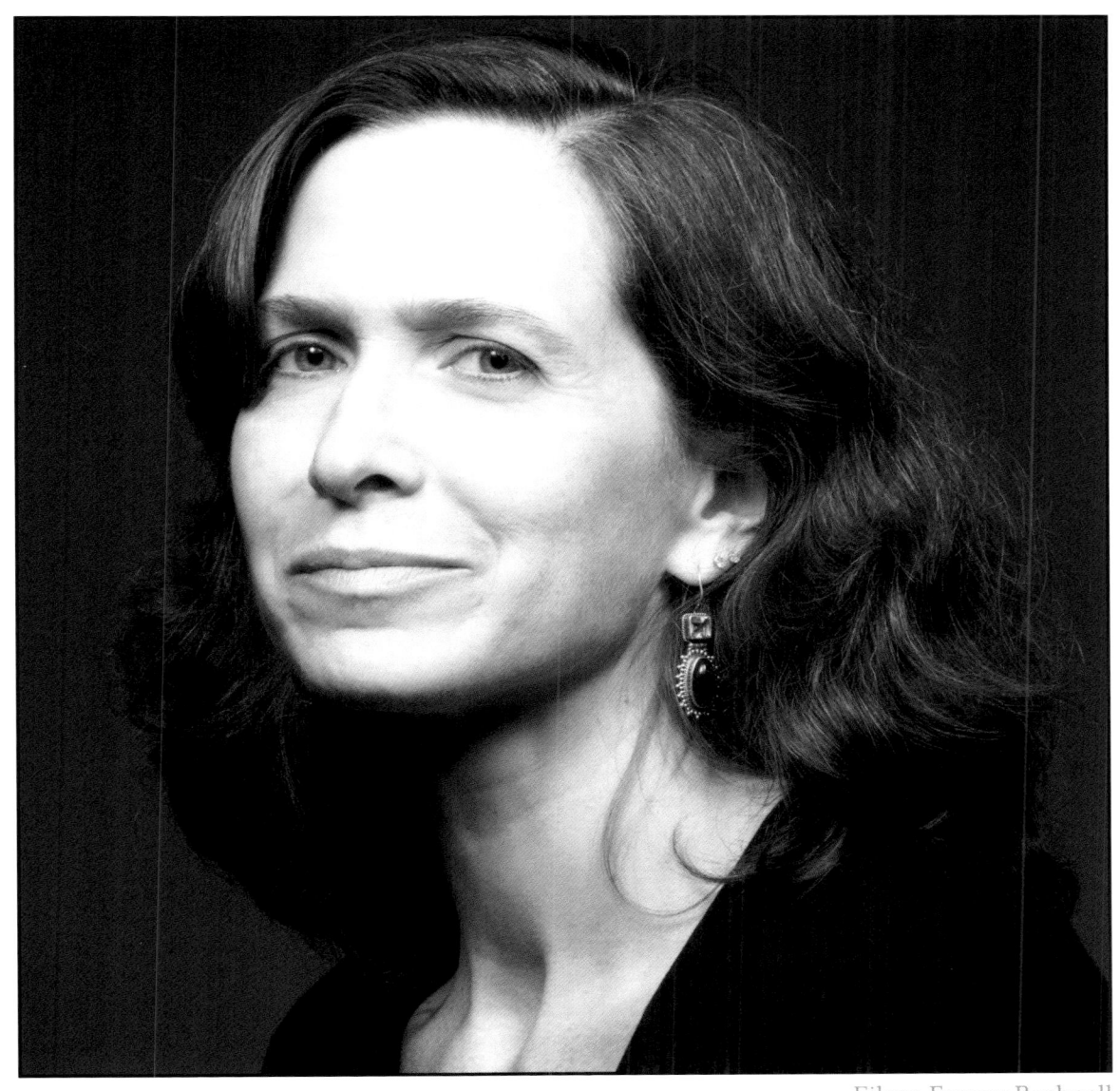

Eileen Feeney Bushnell

twinned and twinged

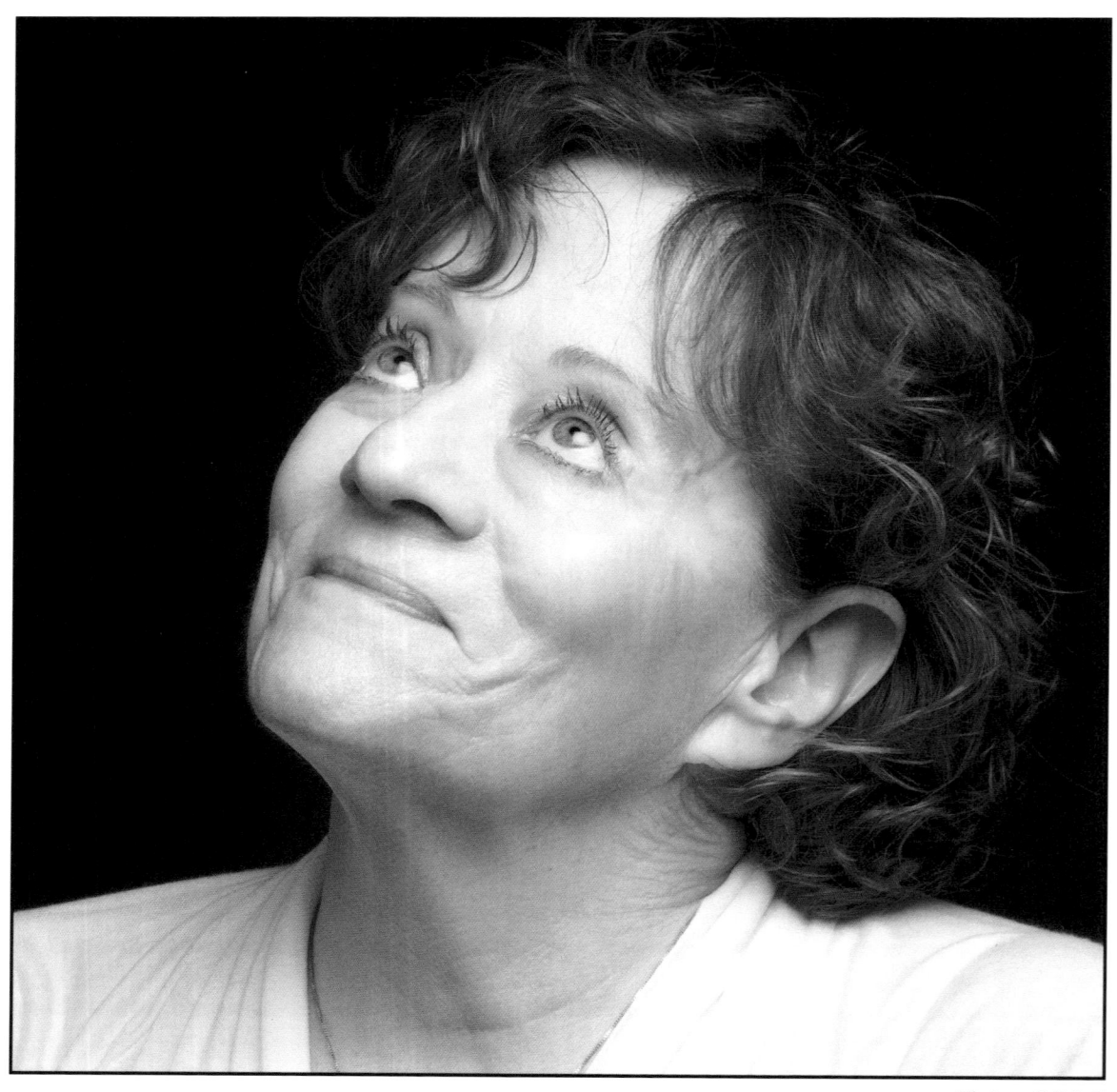

Elaine O'Neil

cast skyward

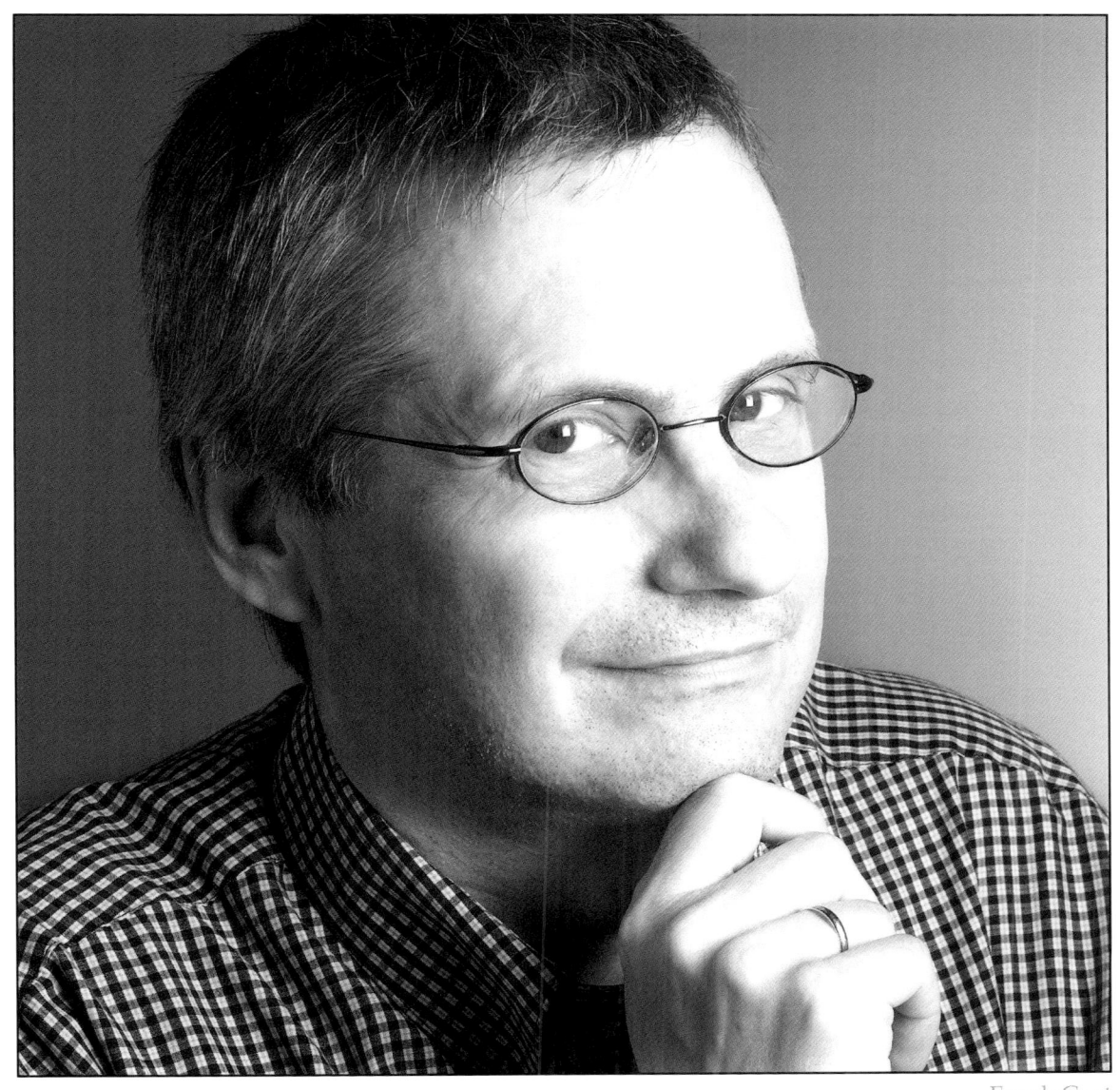

Frank Cost

dreaming of flight.

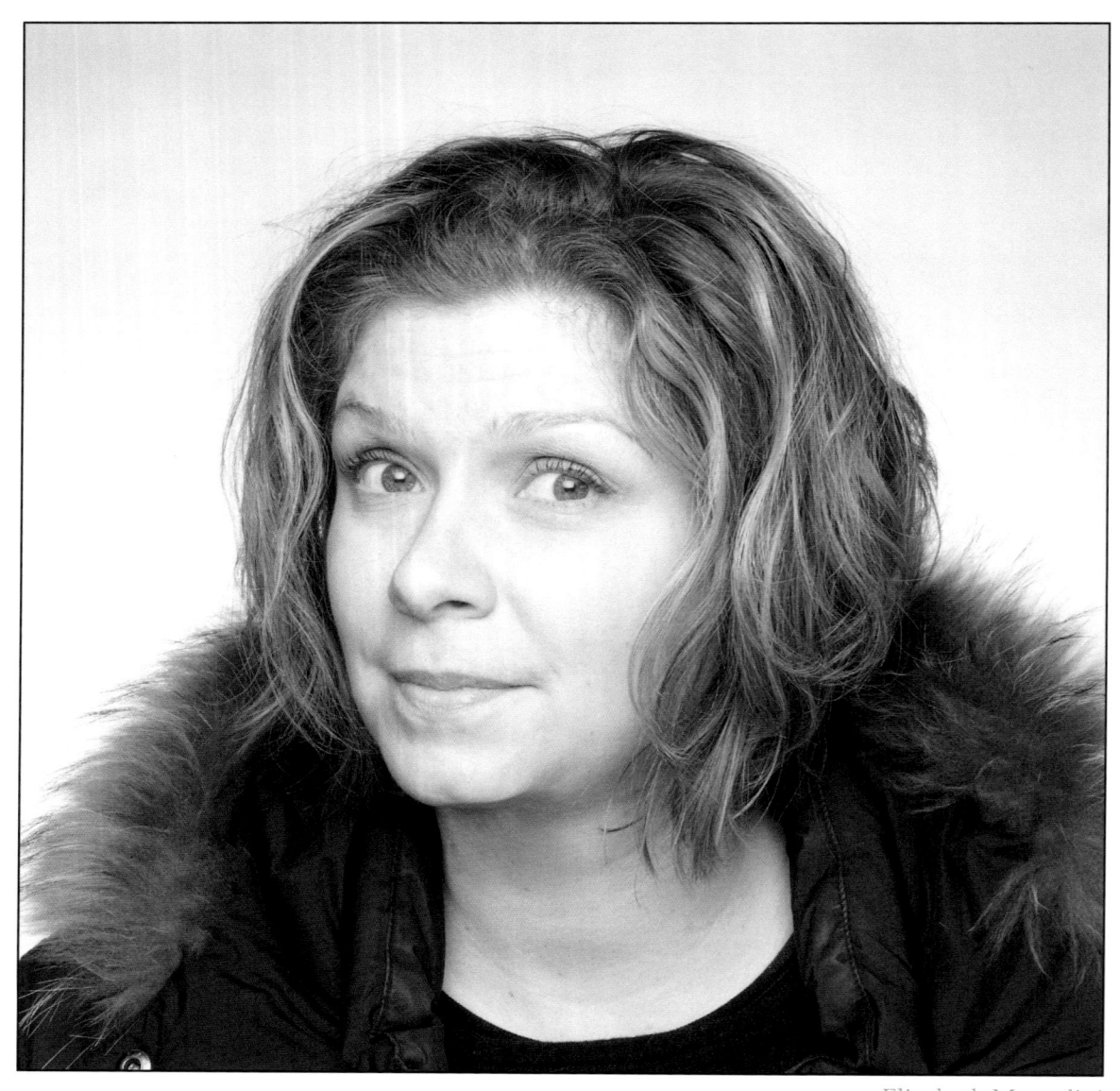

Elizabeth Mazzolini

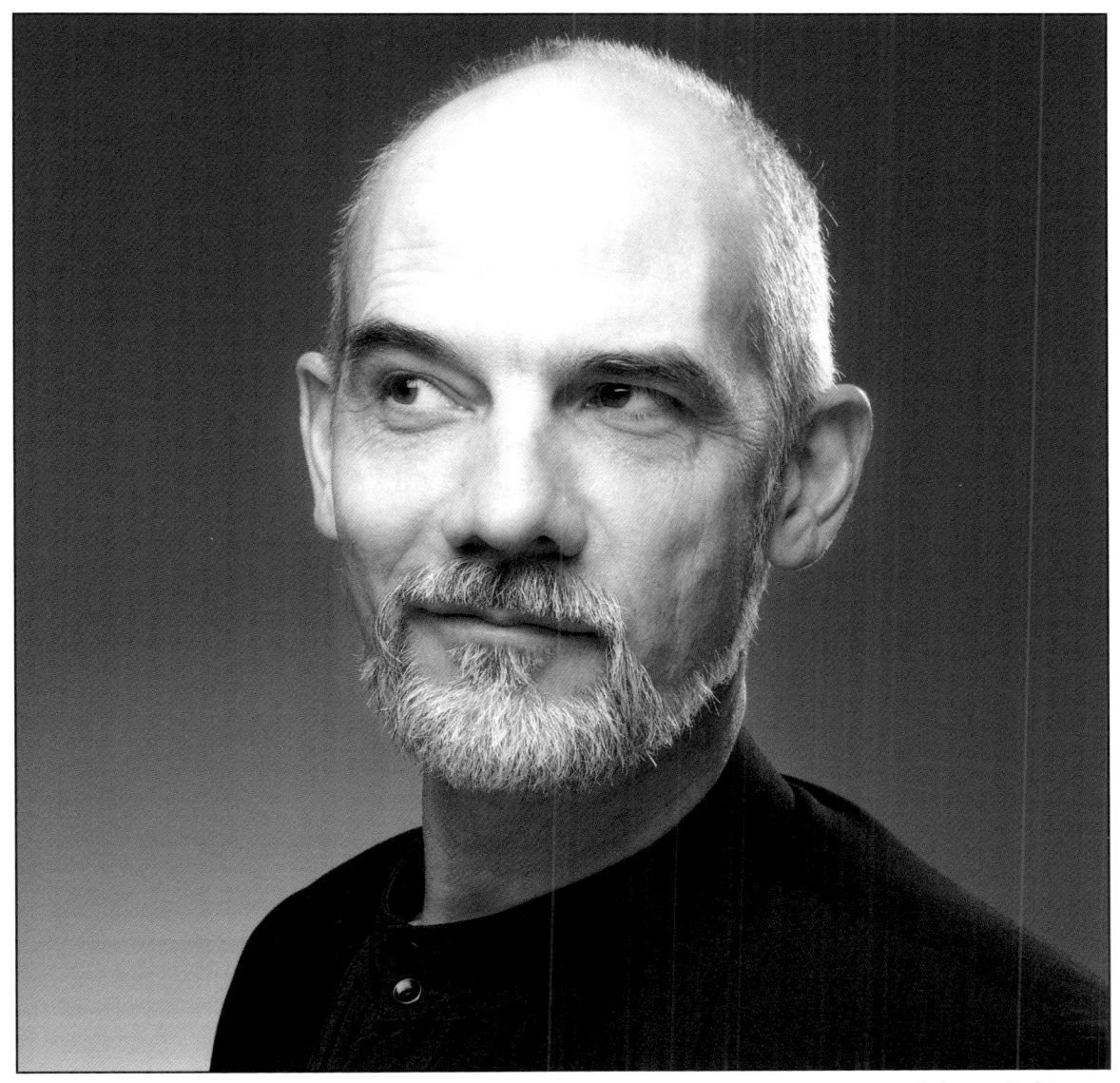

Johnny Robinson

In an instant

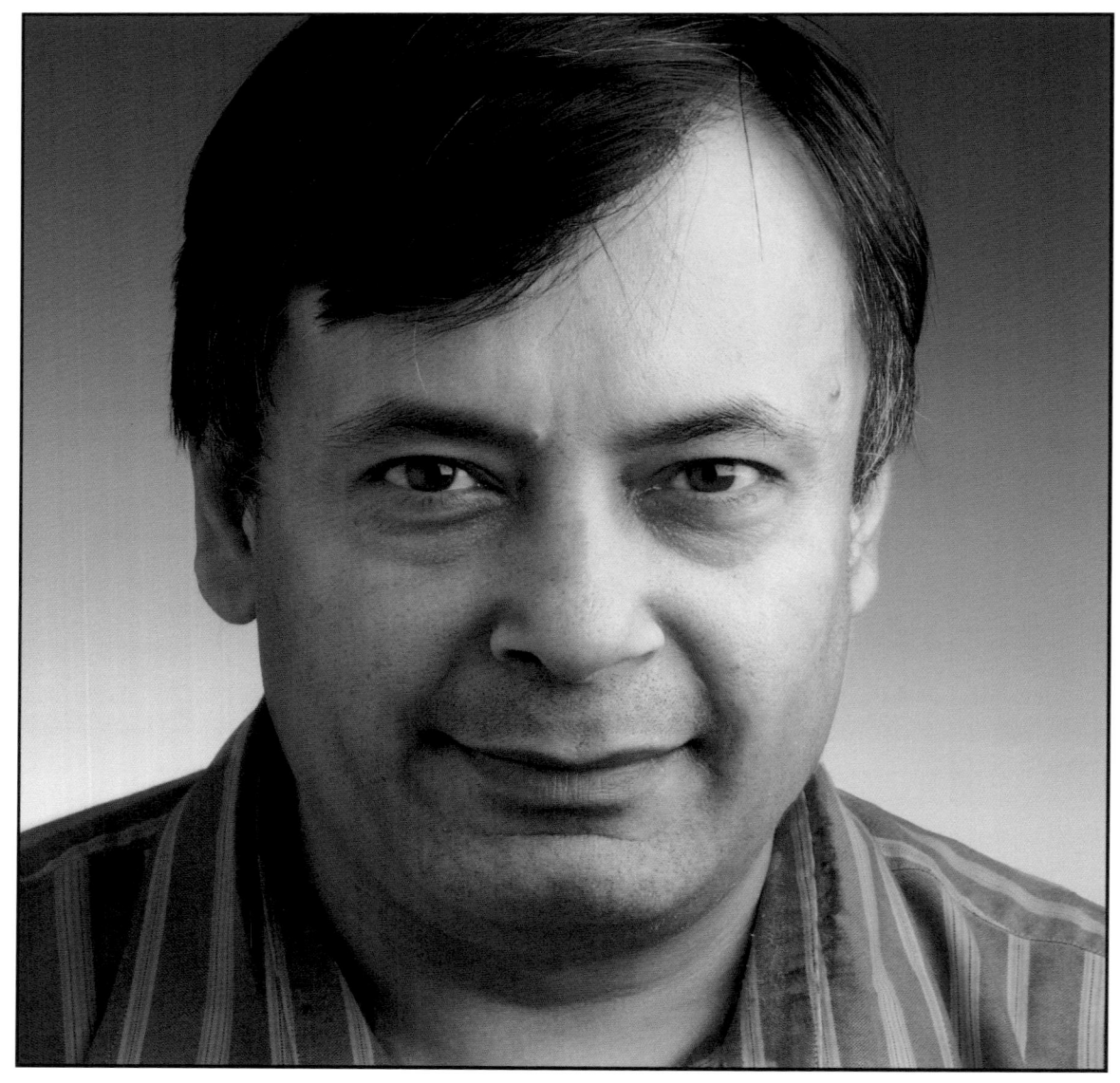

hundreds of instants

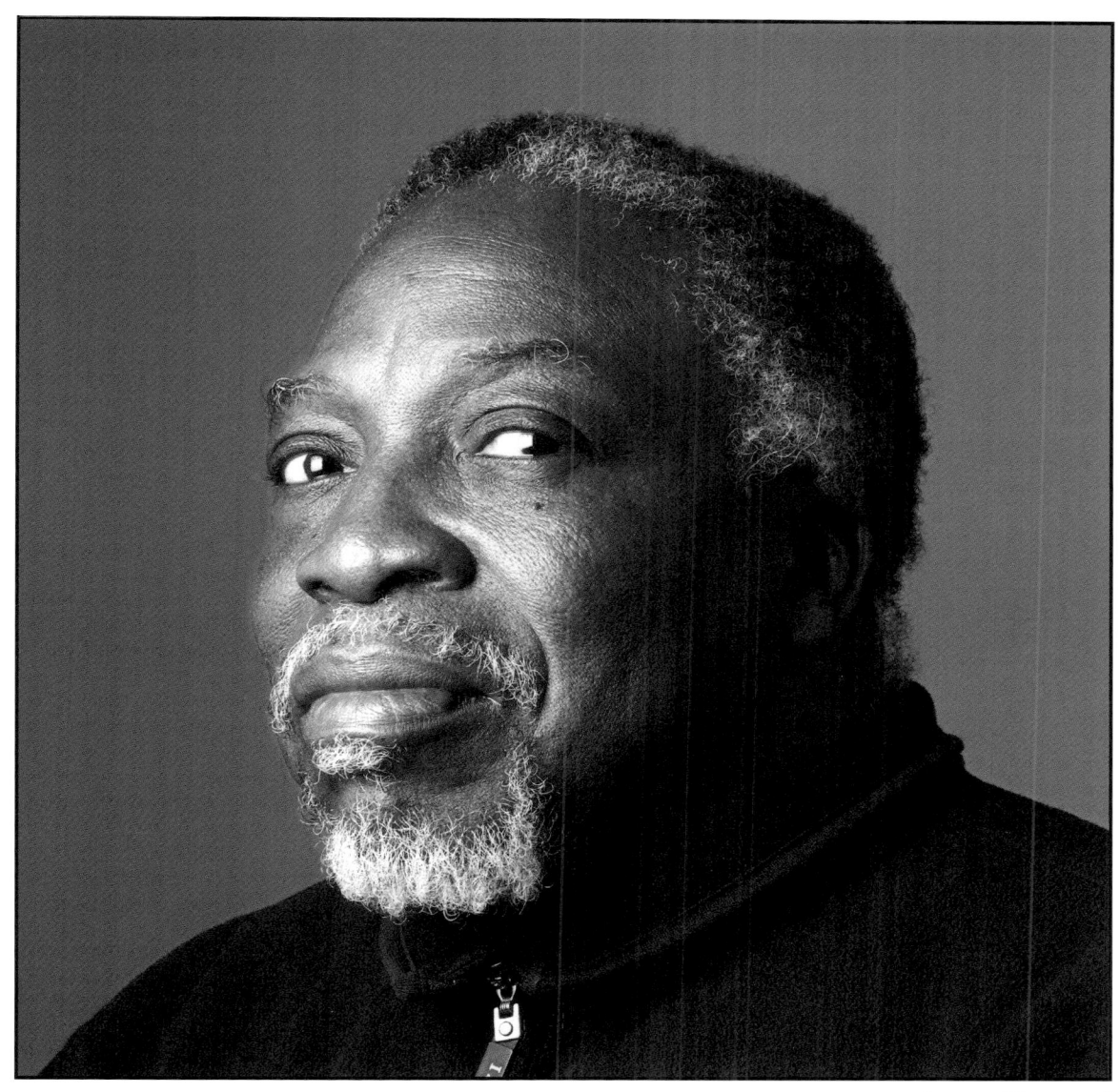

Luvon Sheppard

the photographer hunts

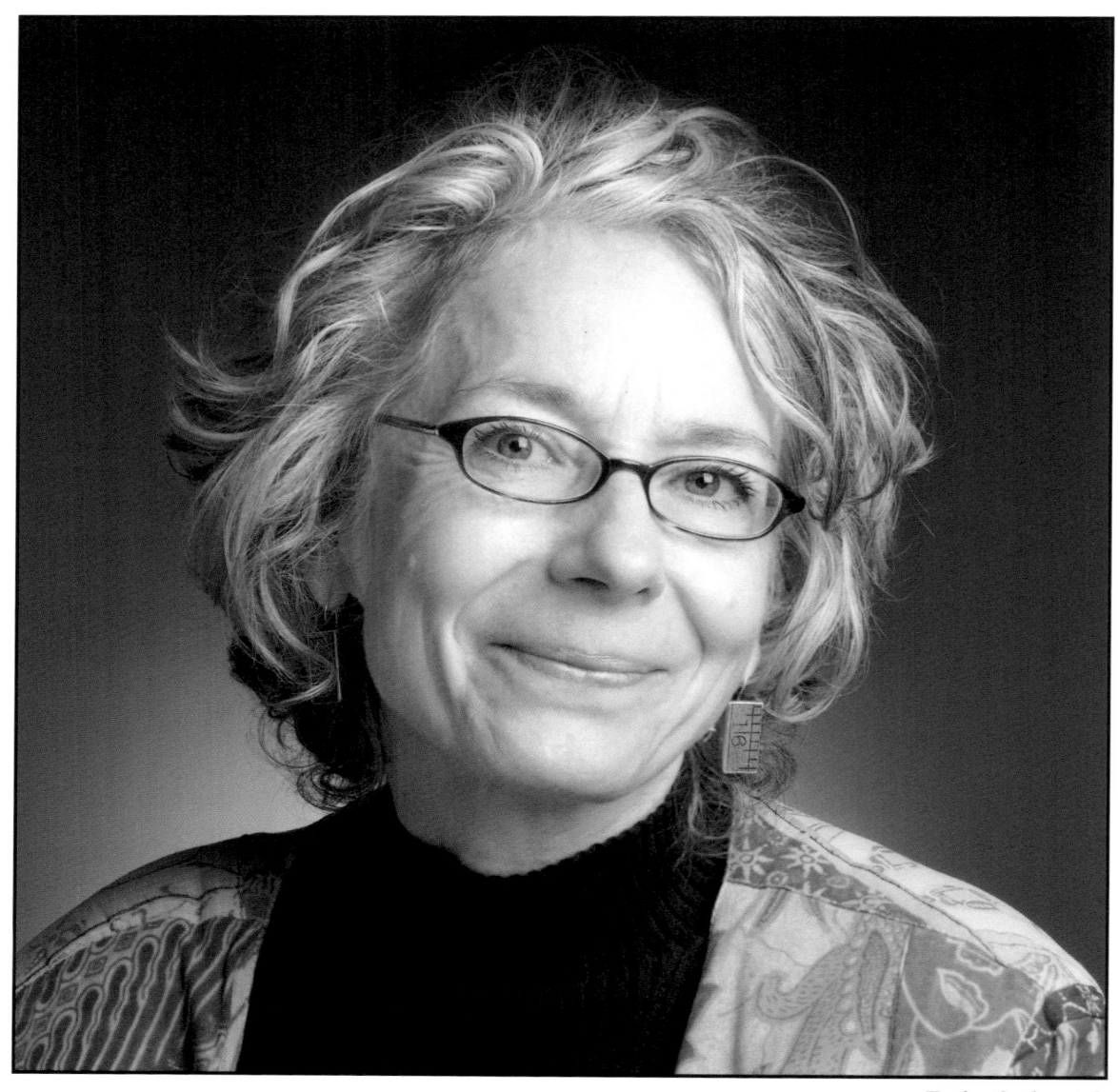

fireflies in the dark

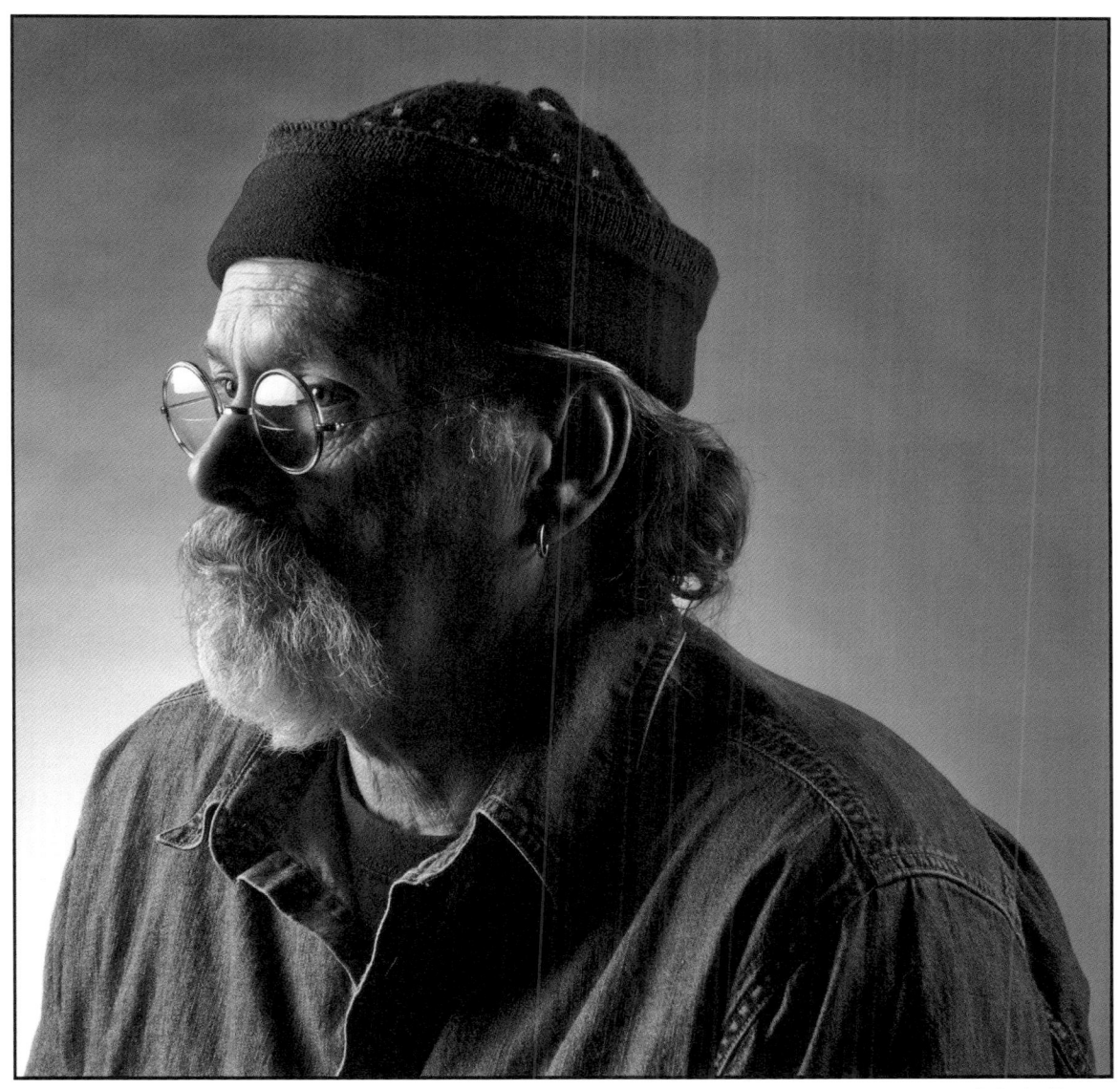

G.S. DeFoore

snap, catch, hold in a glass.

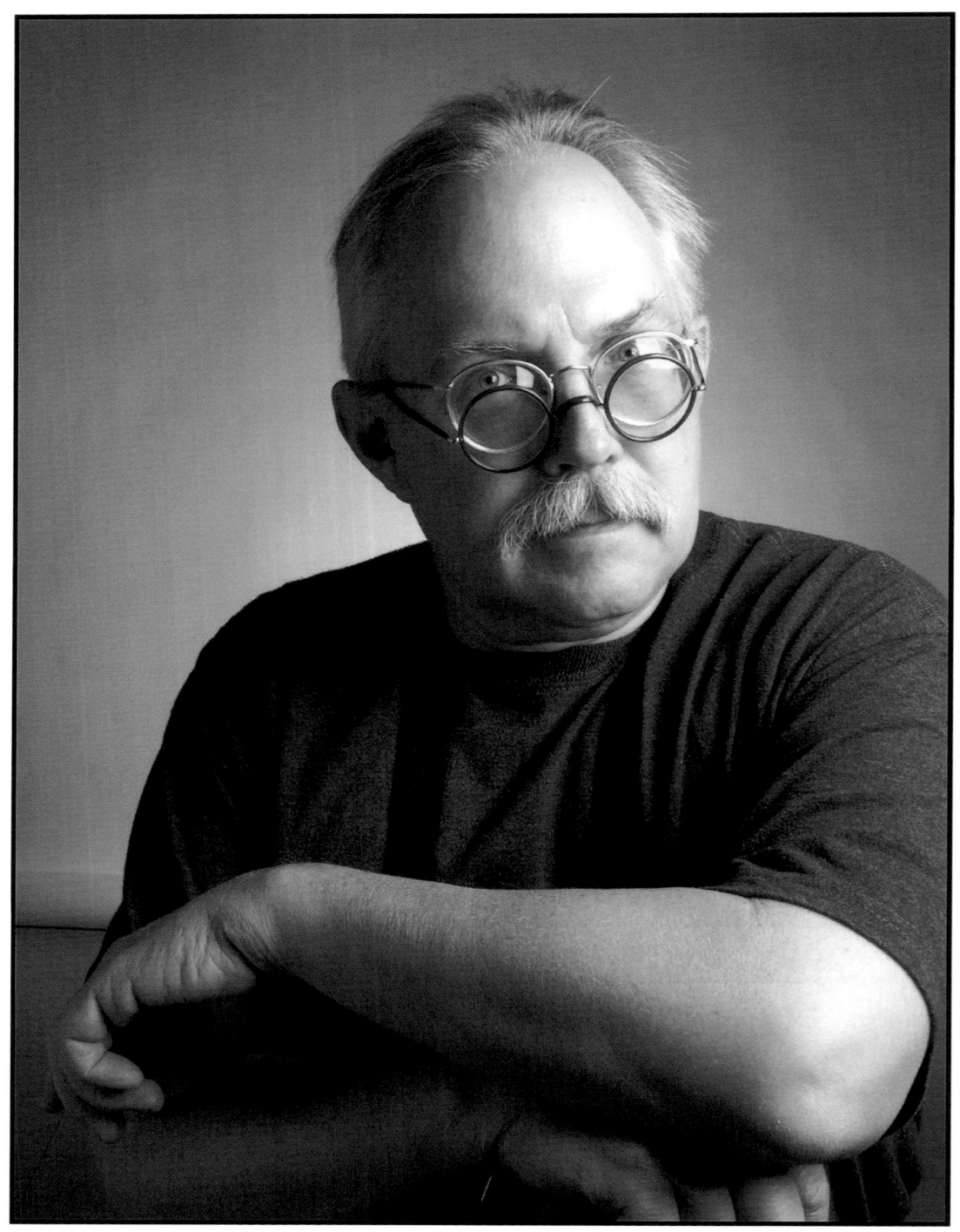

Bill Wadeikis

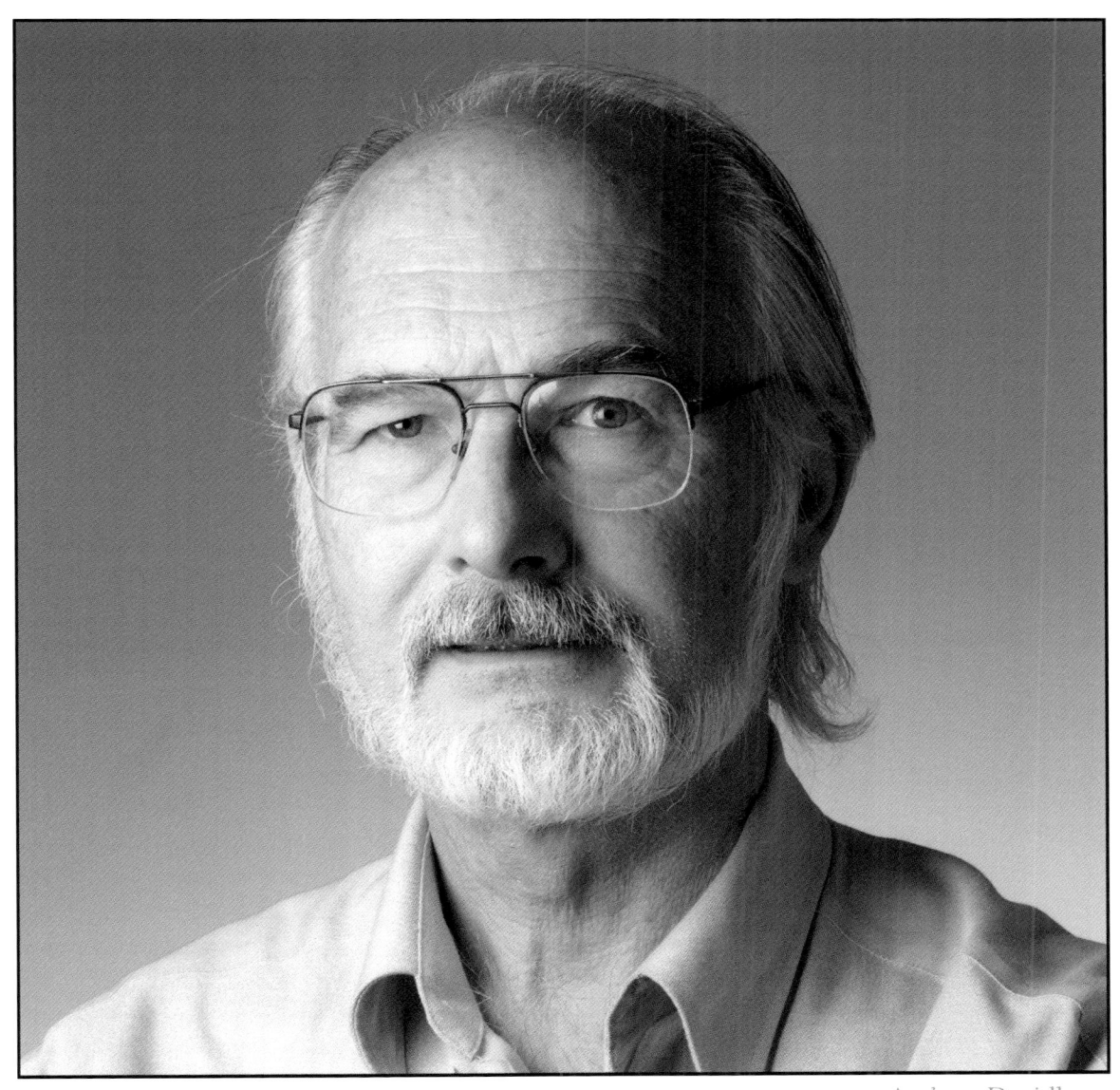

The pearls of a formulated phrase

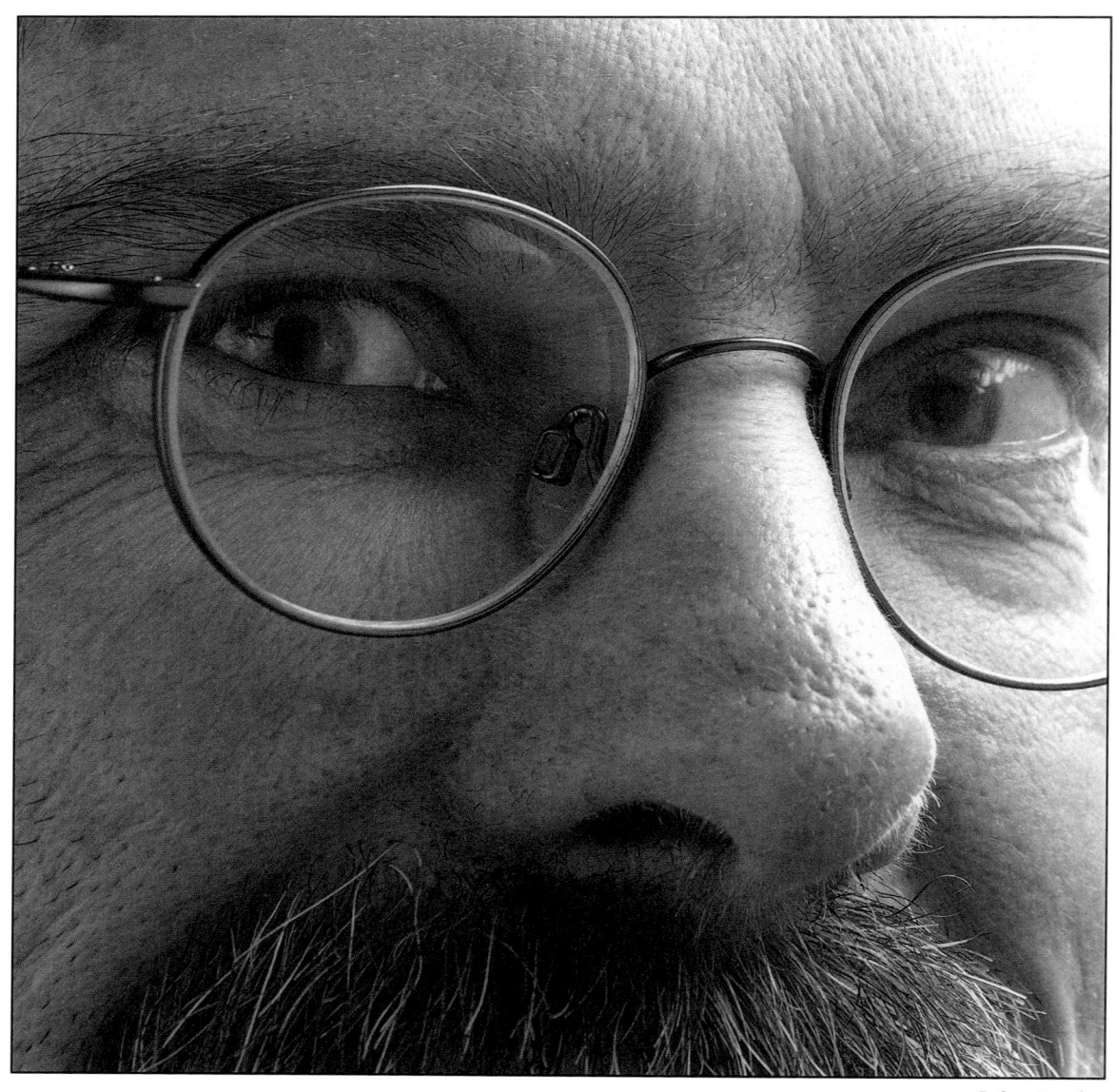

John Roche

the eyes have it

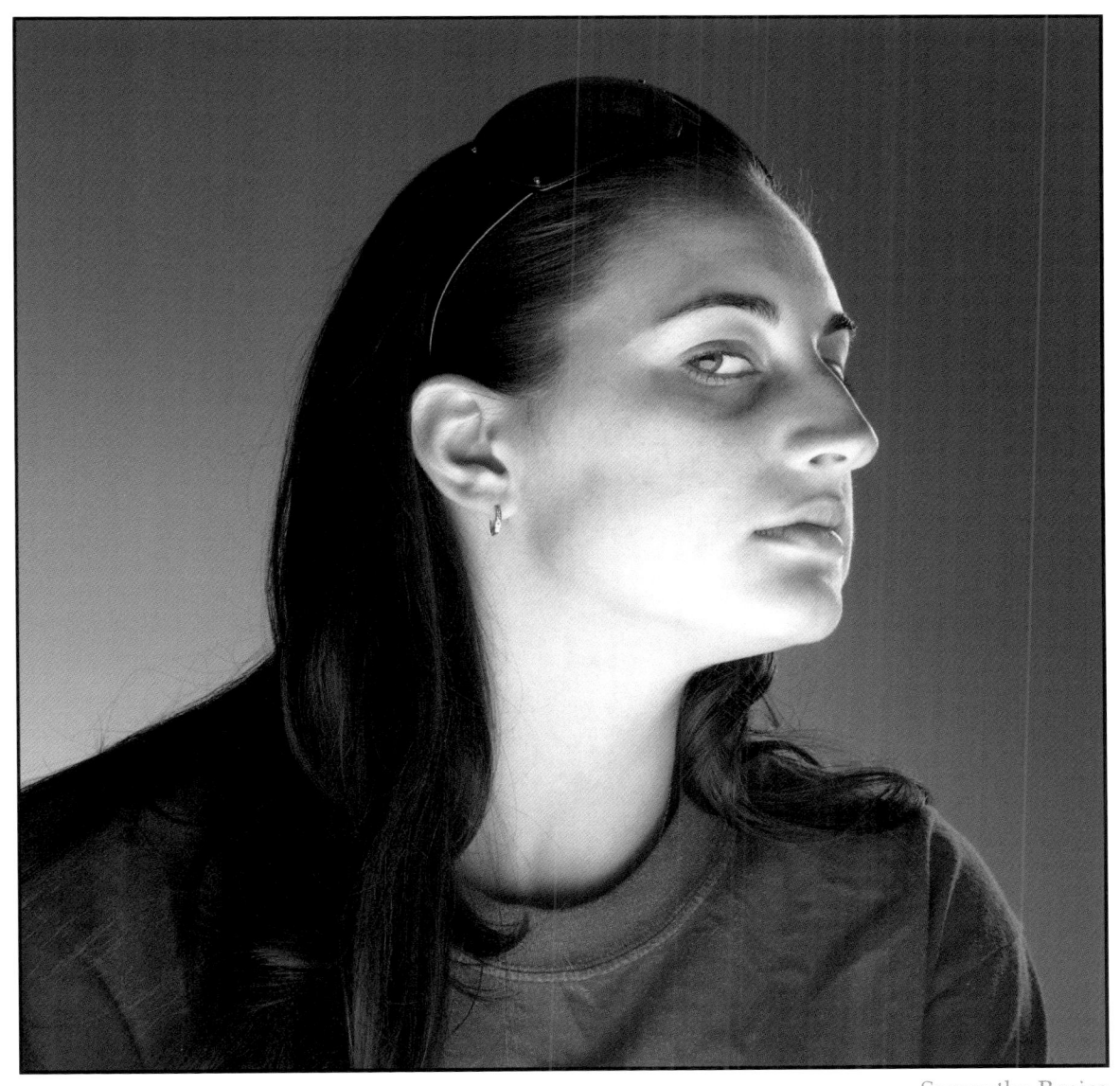

Samantha Bosica

keep one on you

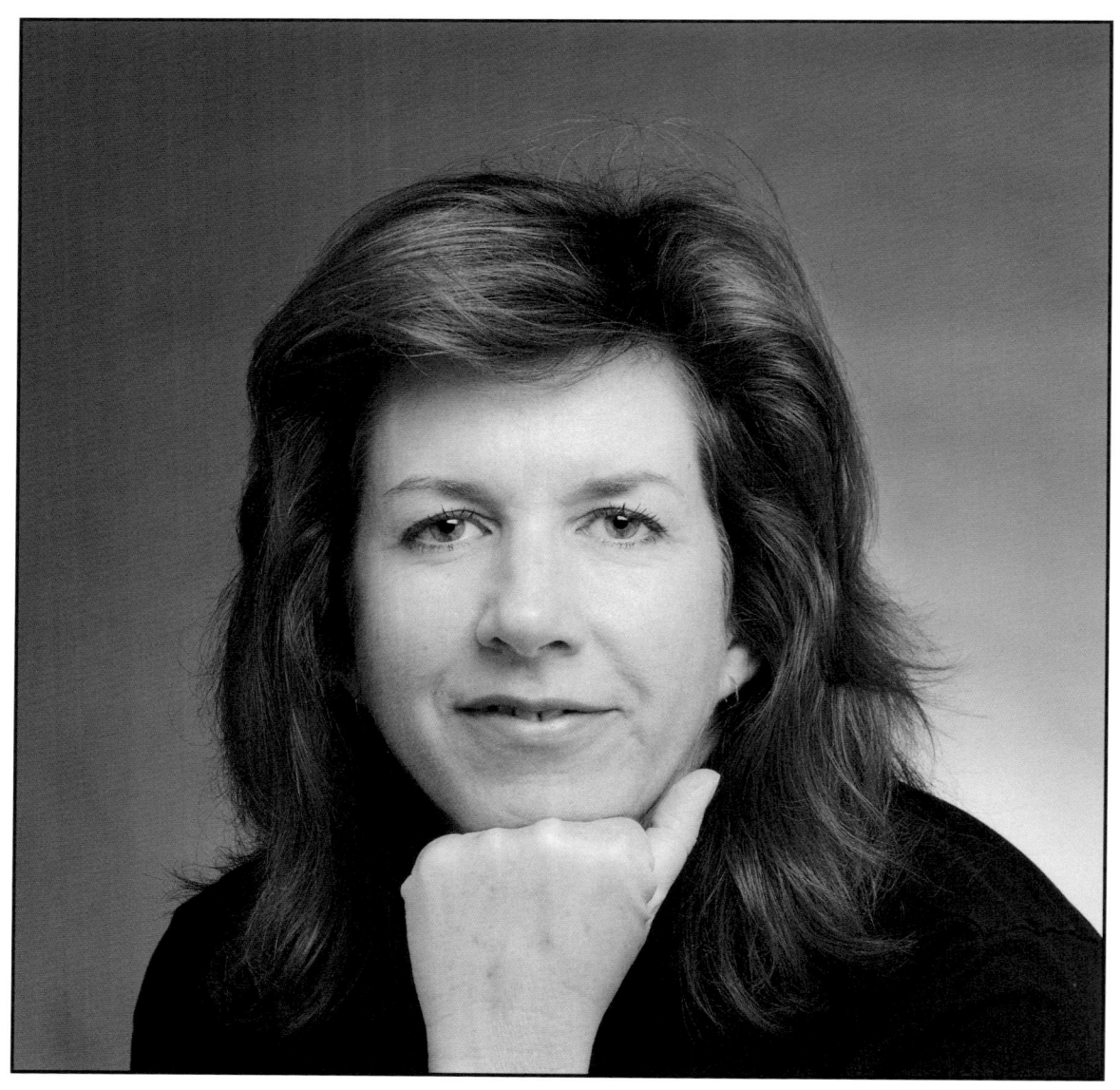

Susan Lakin

brown eyes, black eyes

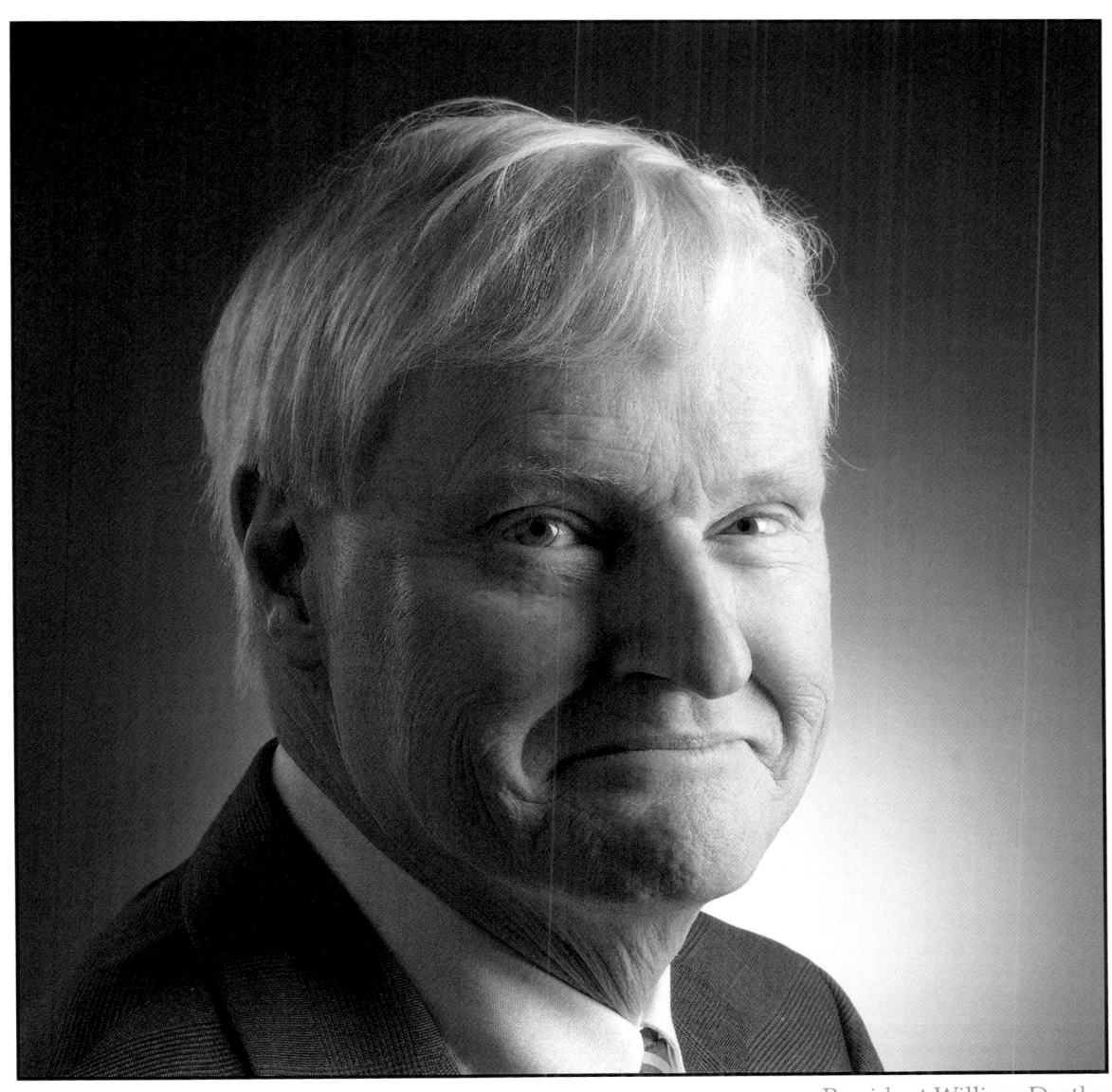

President William Destler

green and blue eyes,

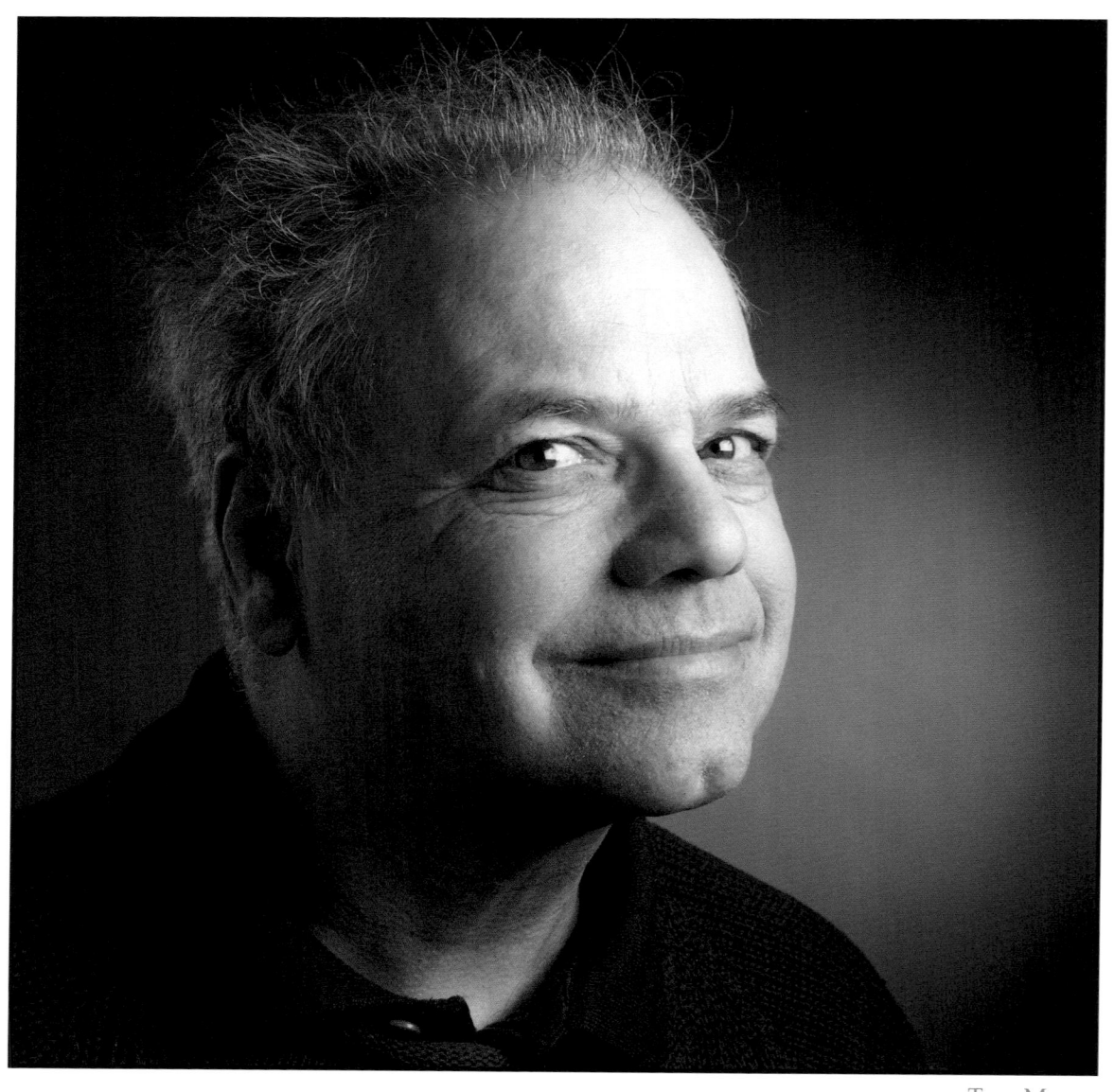

Tom Moran

in the headlights, eyes.

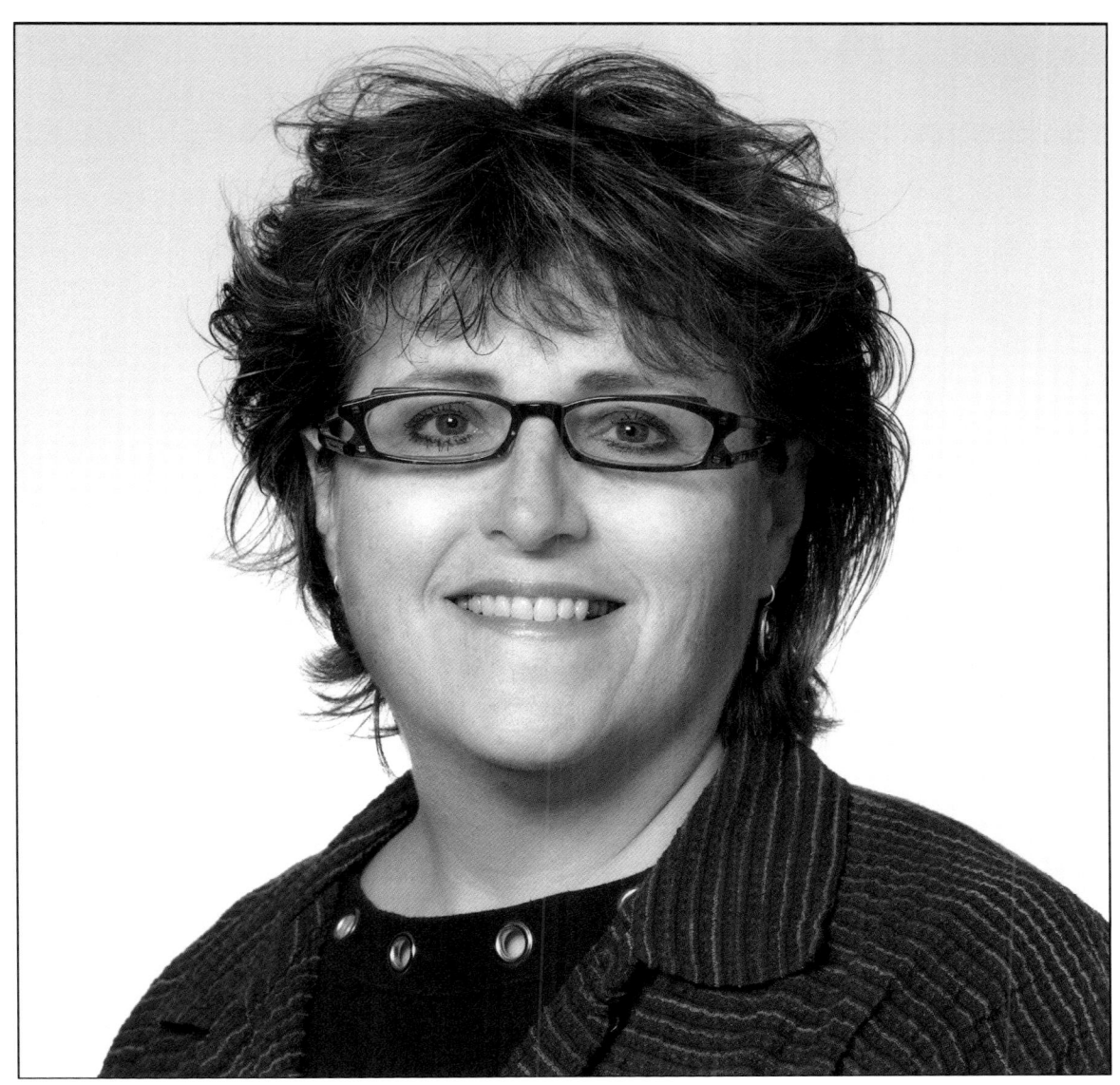

Joyce Hertzson

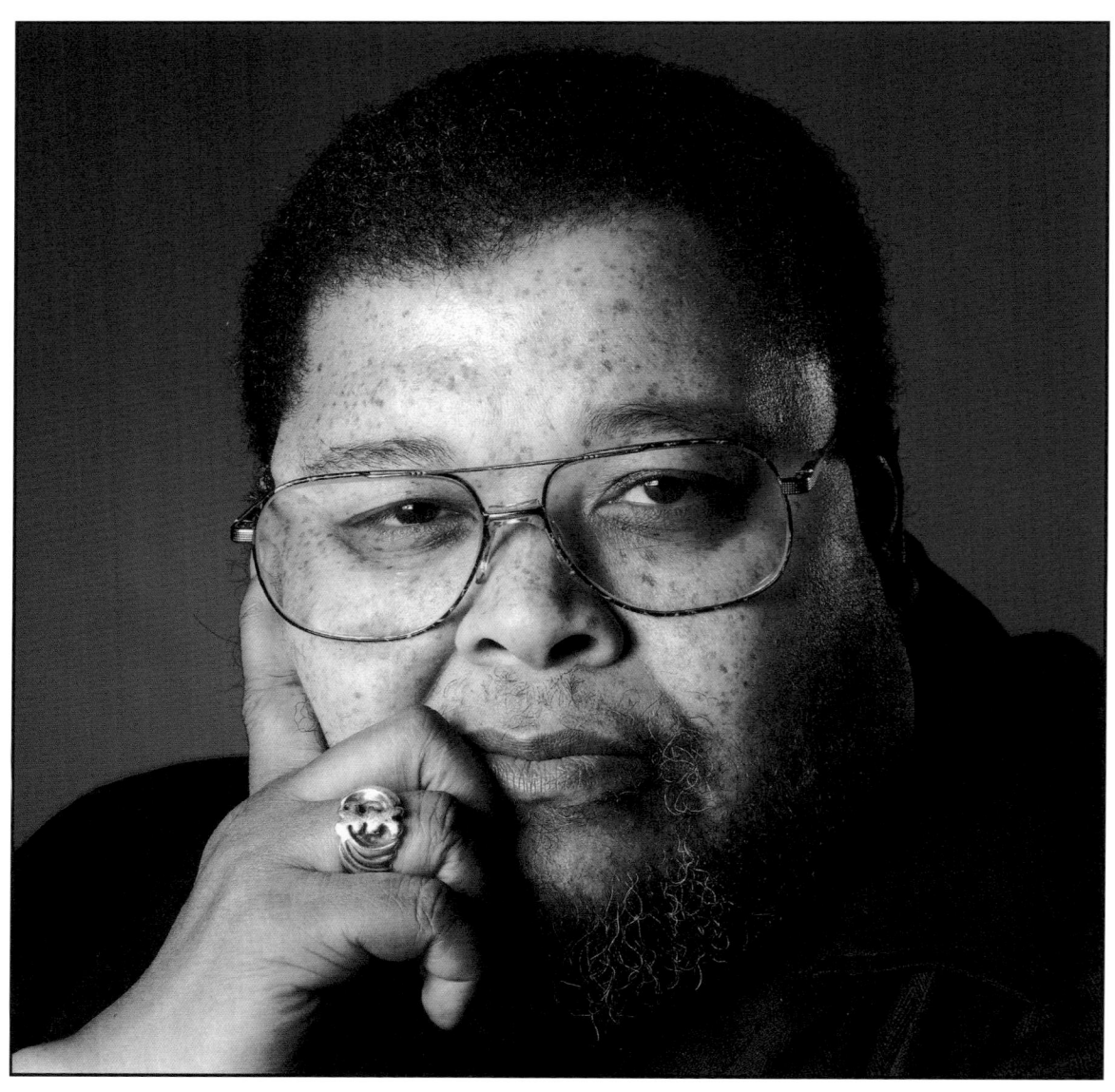

Vincent F.A. Golphin

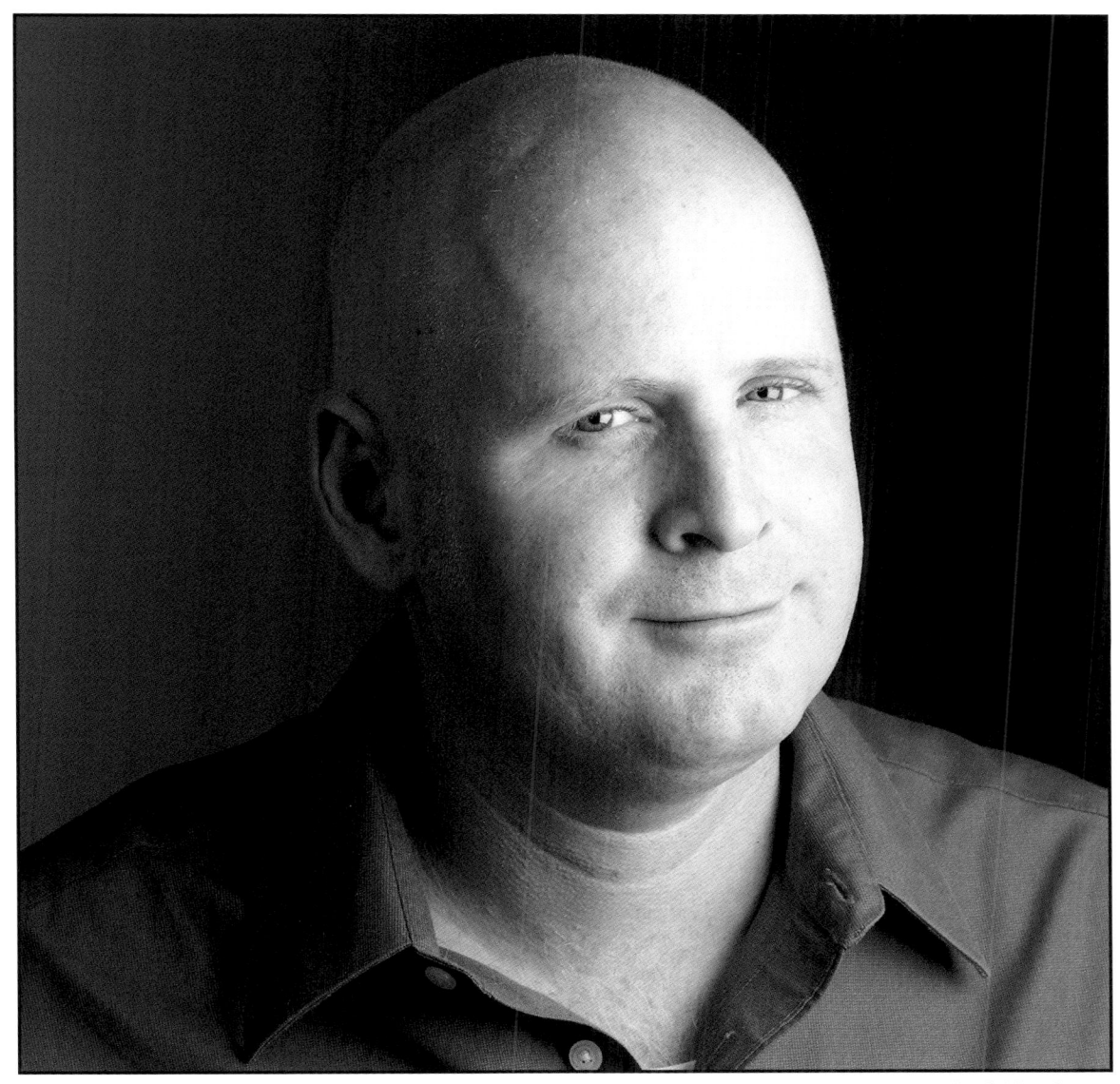

Rod Northcutt

How many tones from white

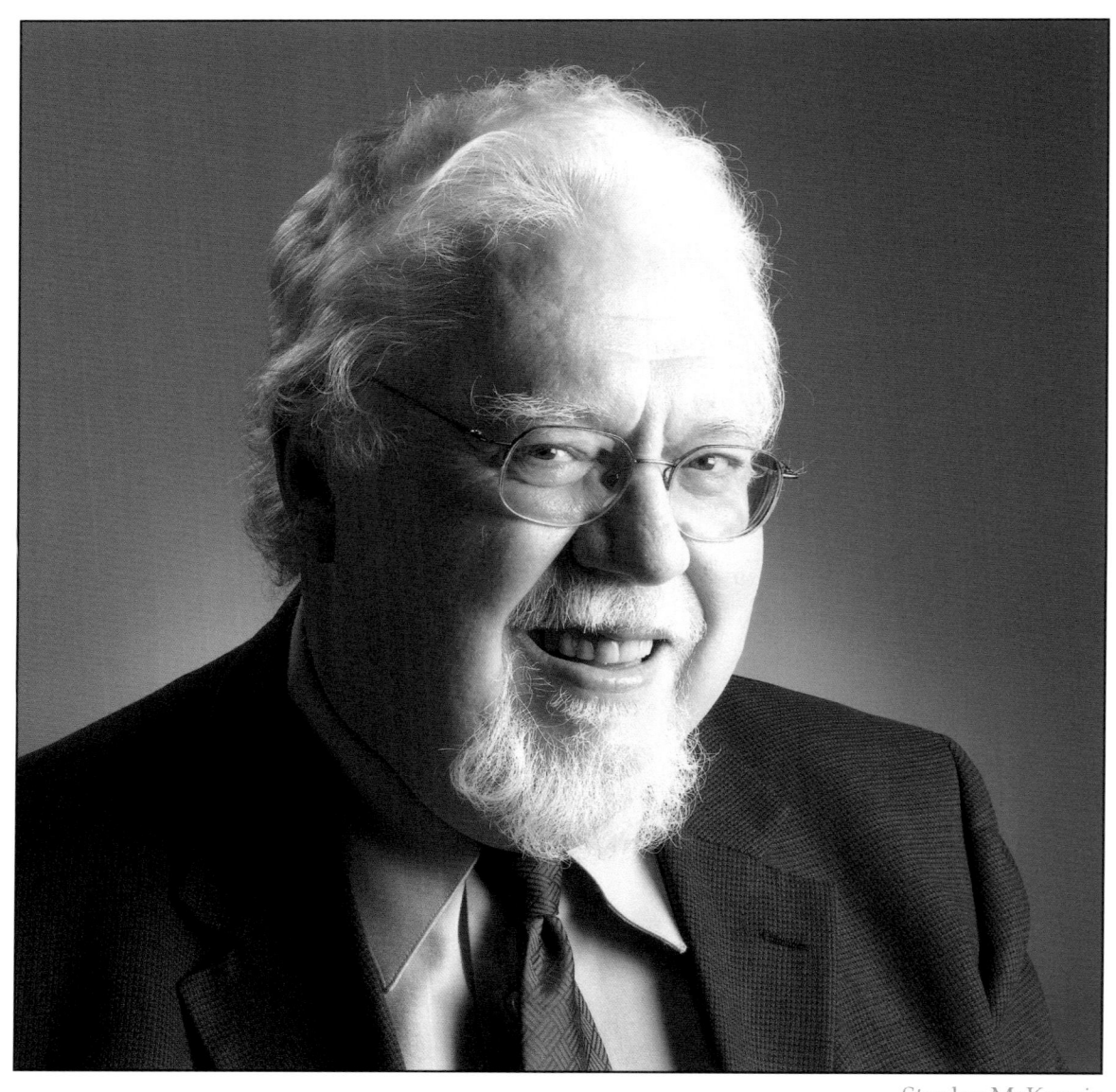

Stanley McKenzie

to black? How many pixels

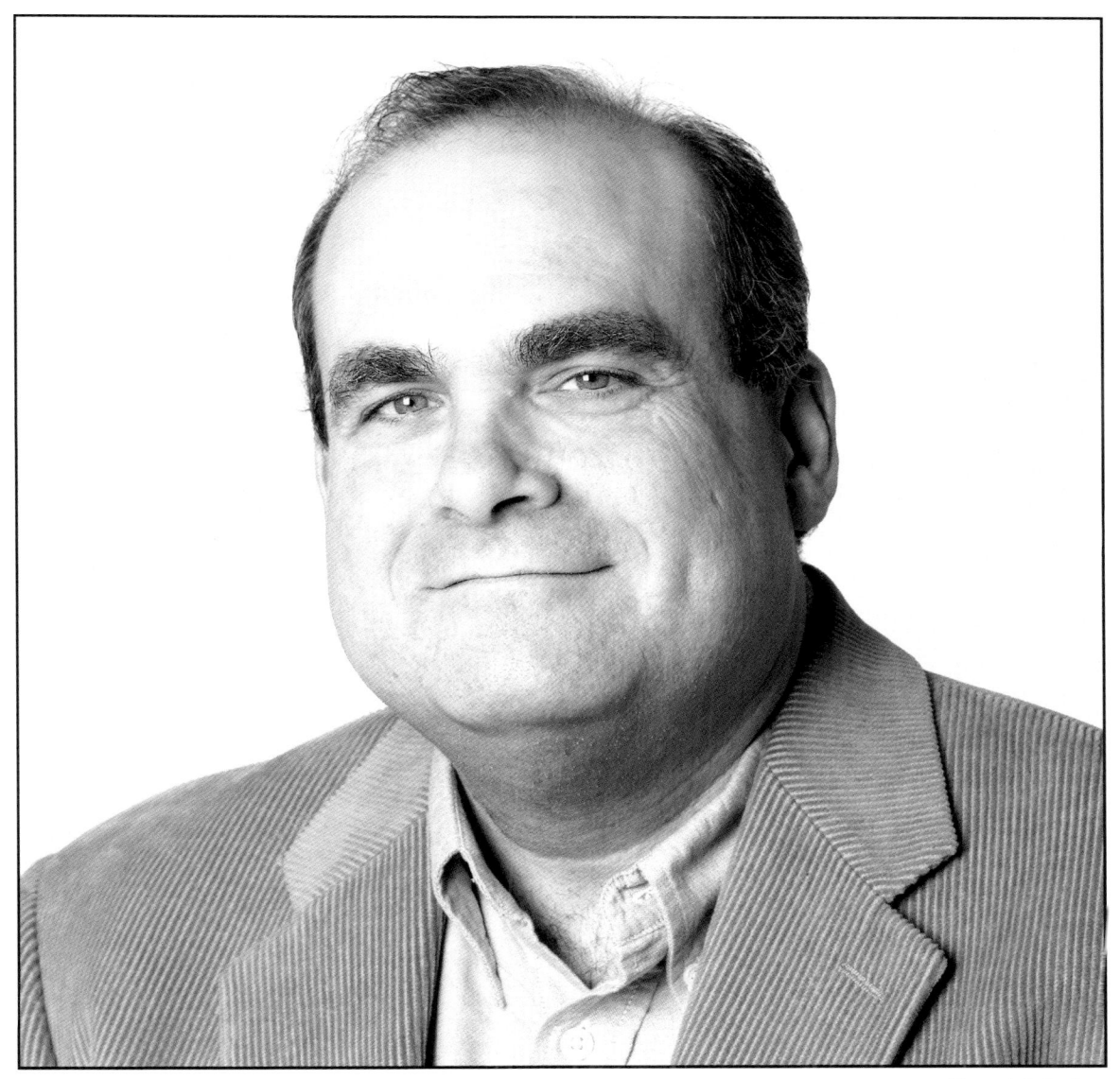

Donald Arday

between shadow and glow?

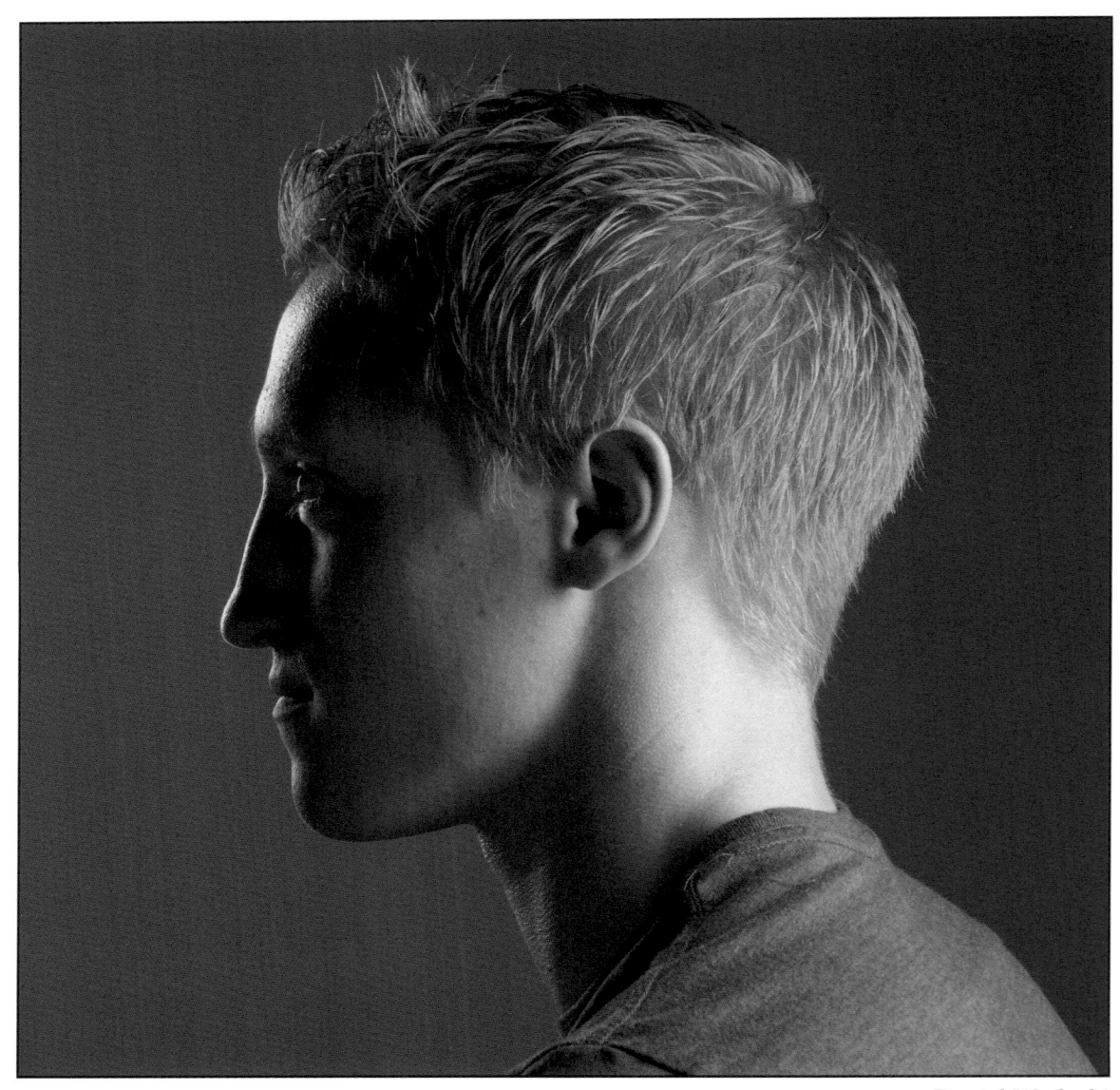

Daniel Wodecki

As many as the fractions

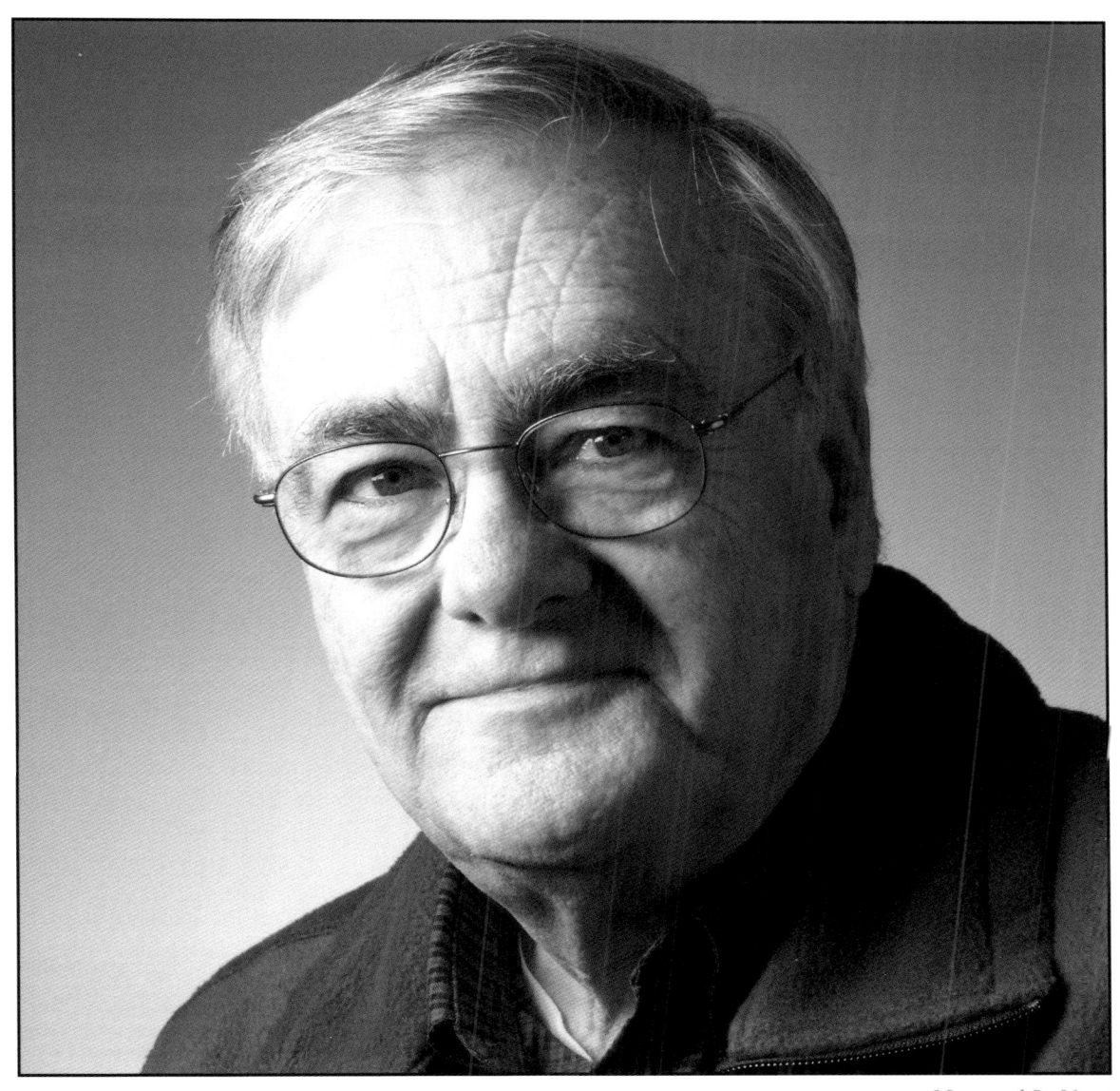

Howard LeVant

of the sitters themselves

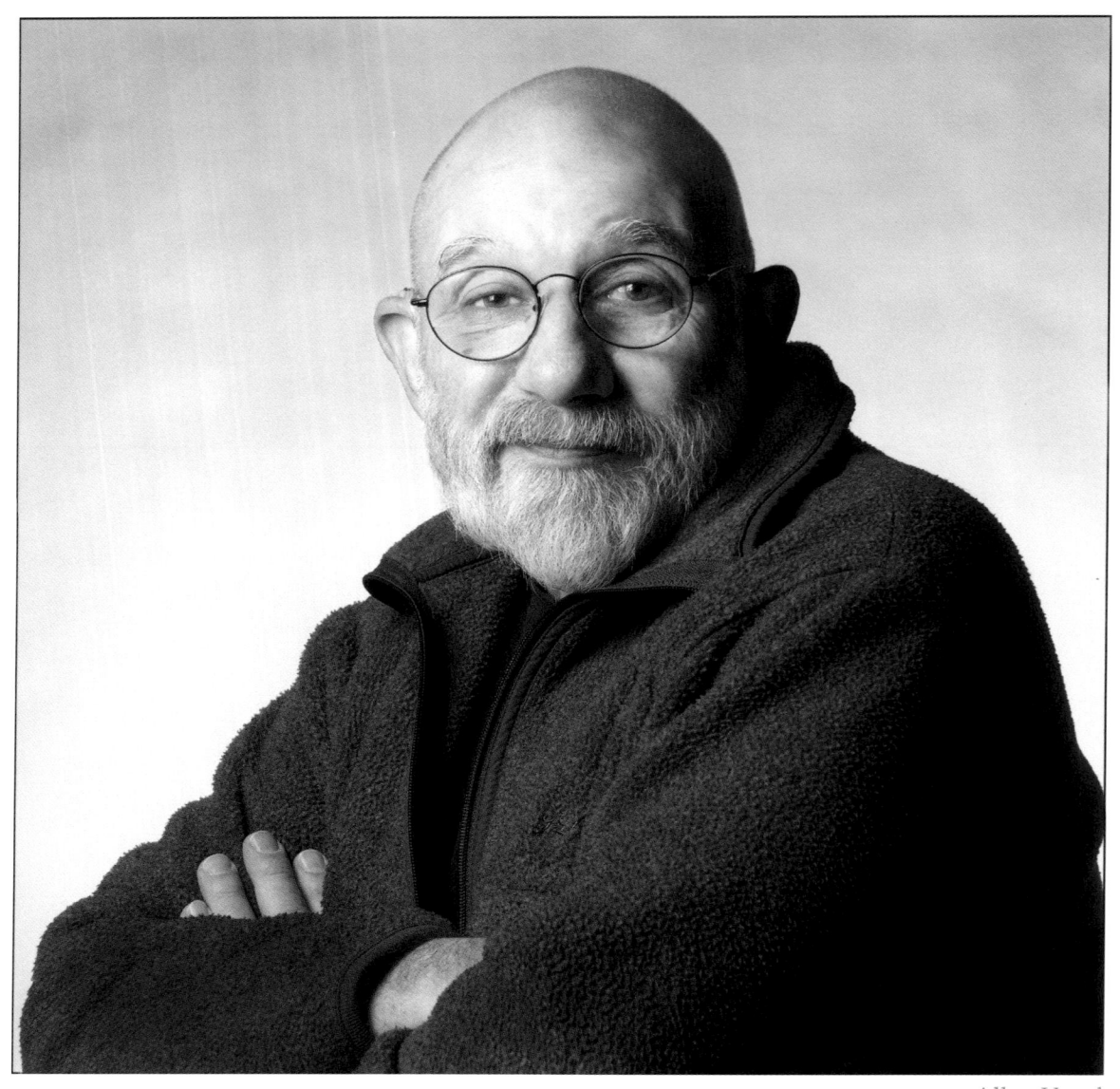

Allen Vogel

countless, unedited,

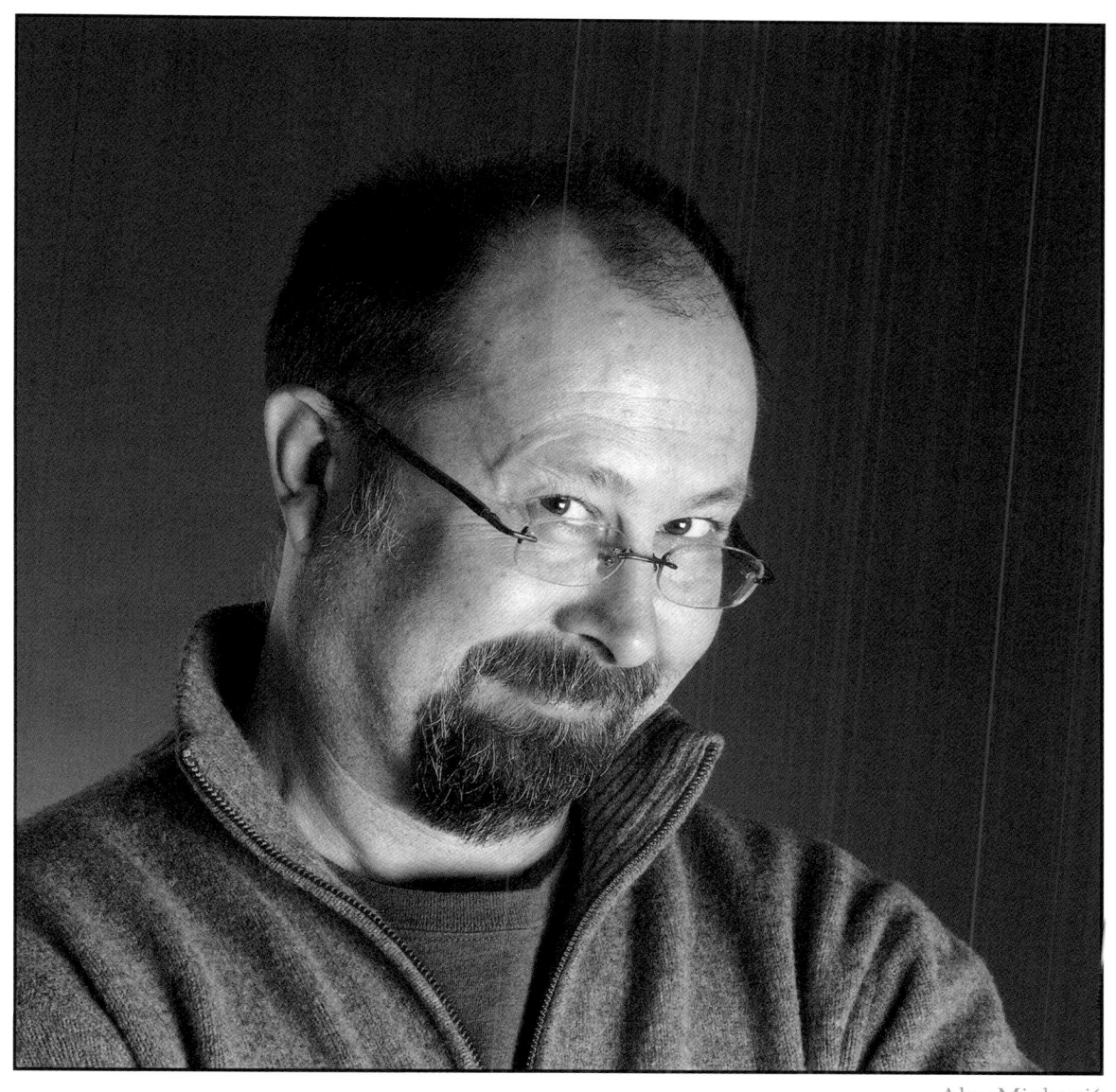

Alex Mioković

caught by a click

David Pankow

faster than thought.

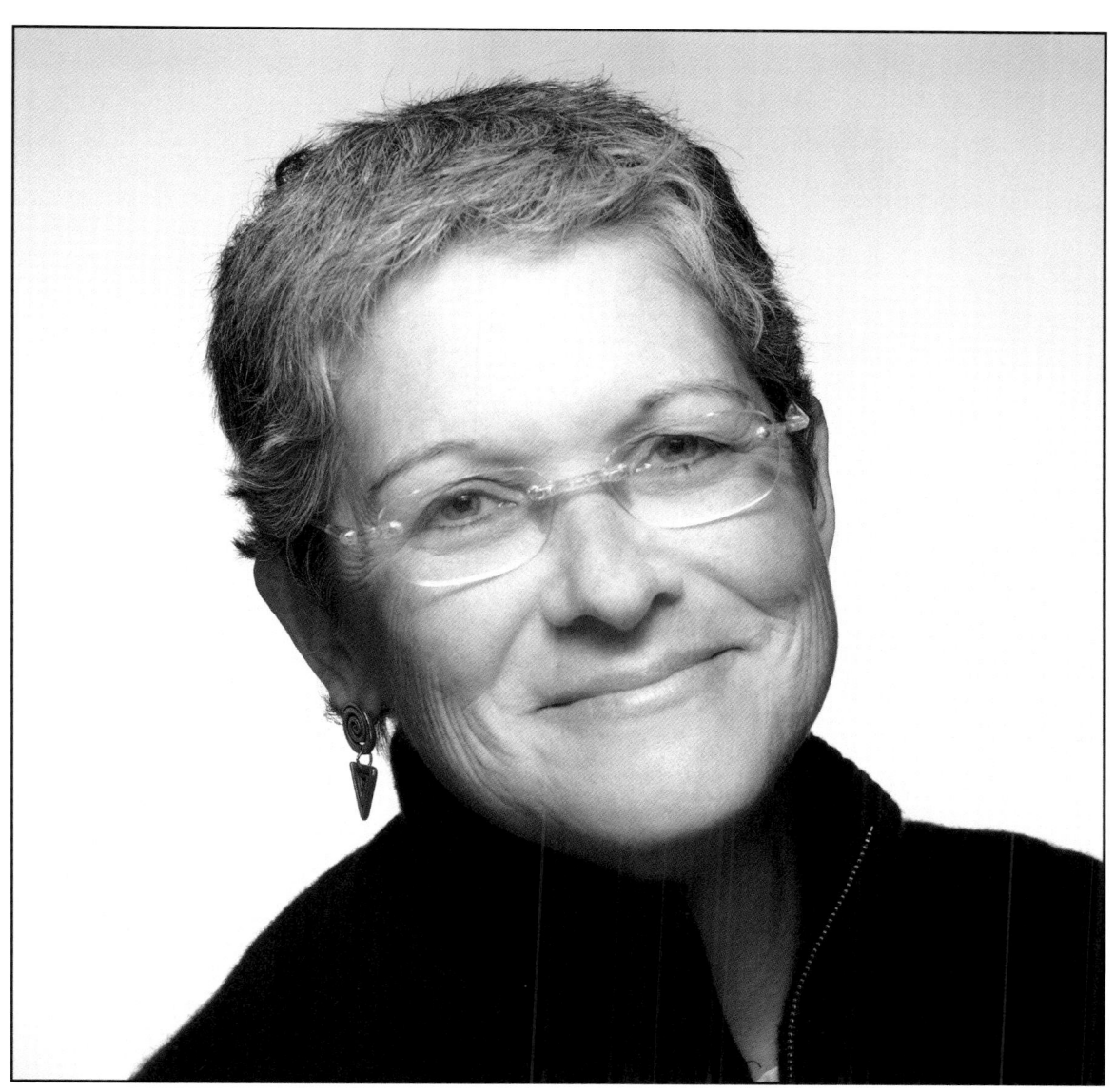

Patti Lachance

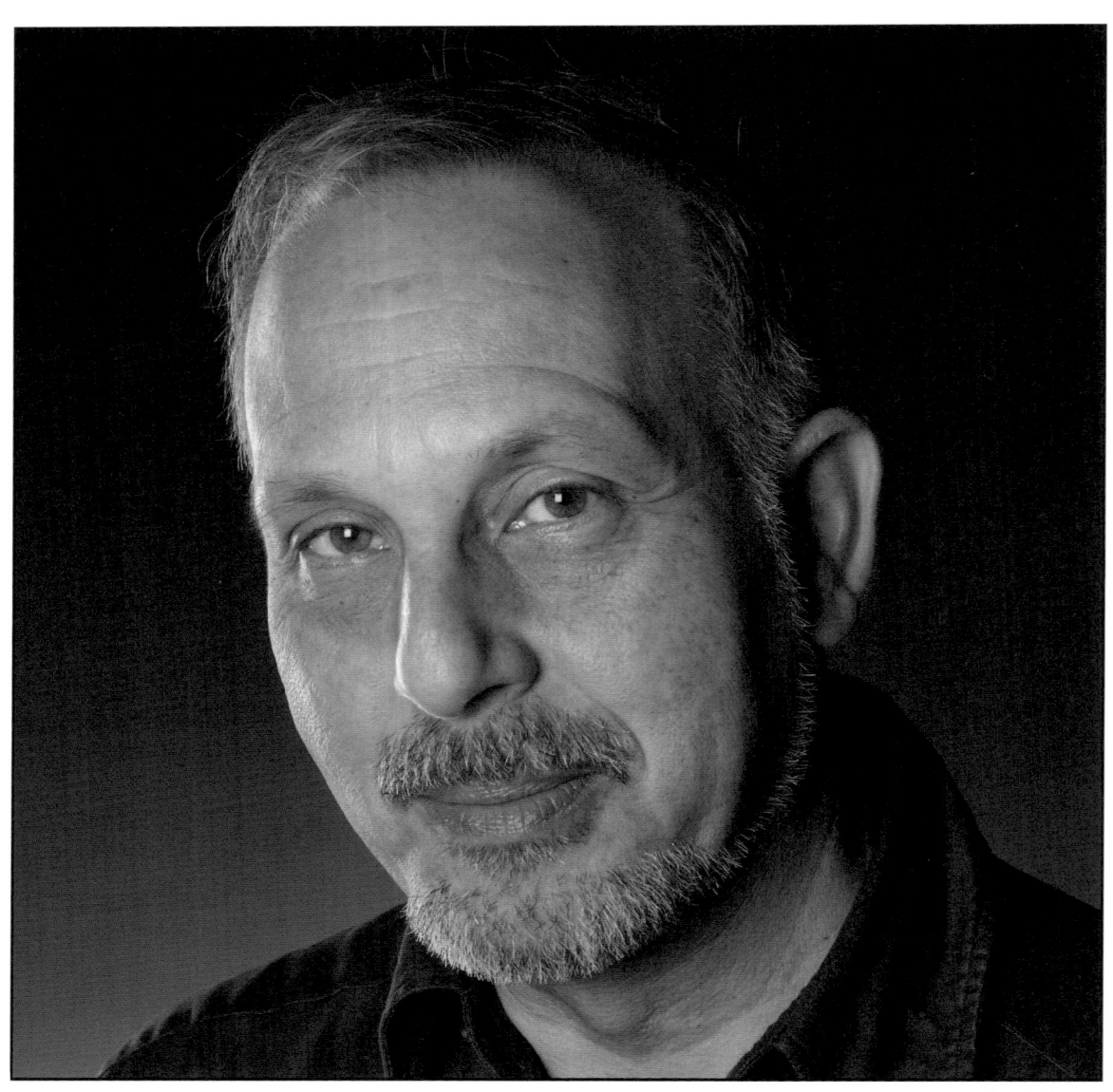

Alan Singer

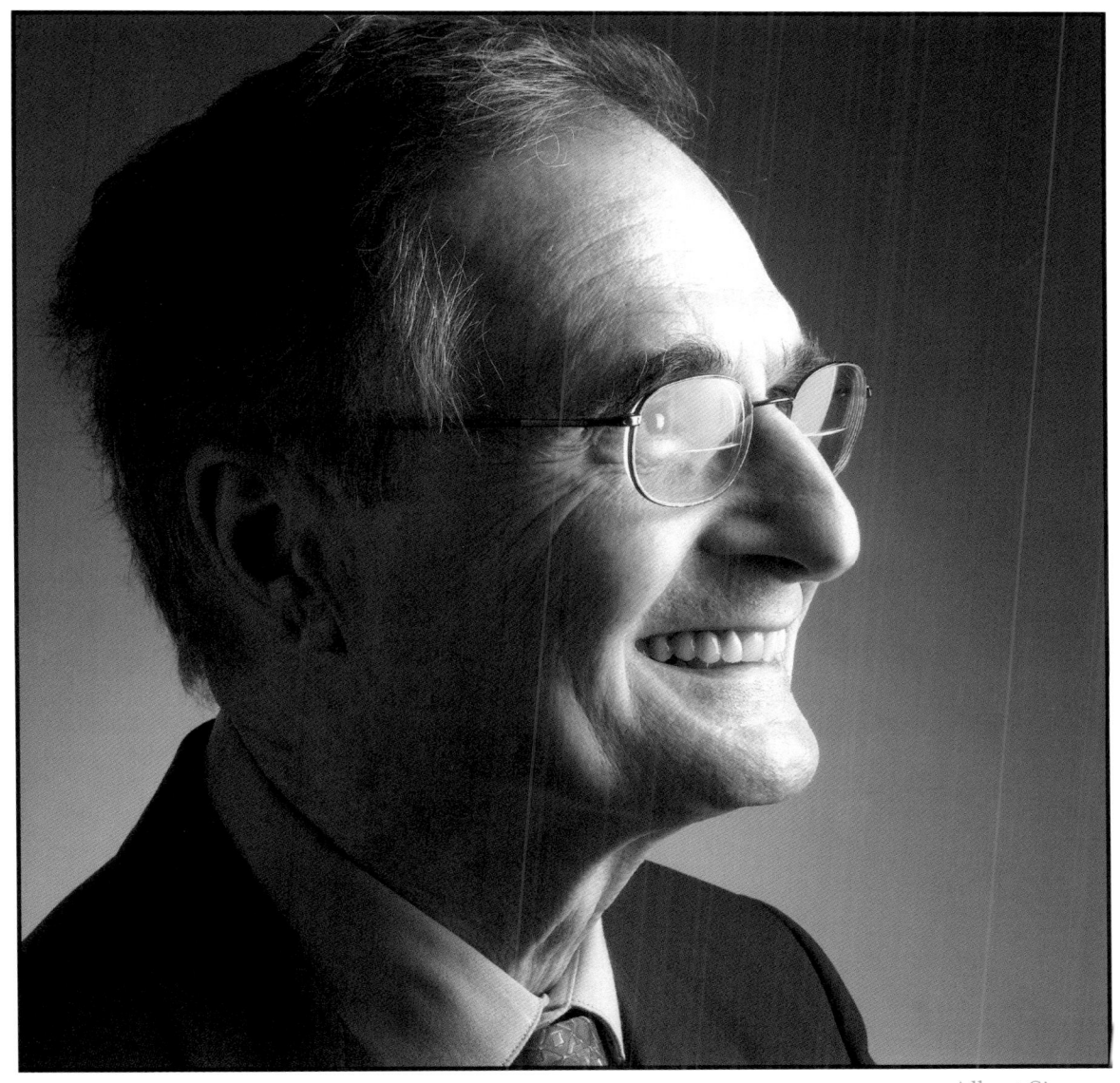

Albert Simone

Come quietly, unburdened, curious.

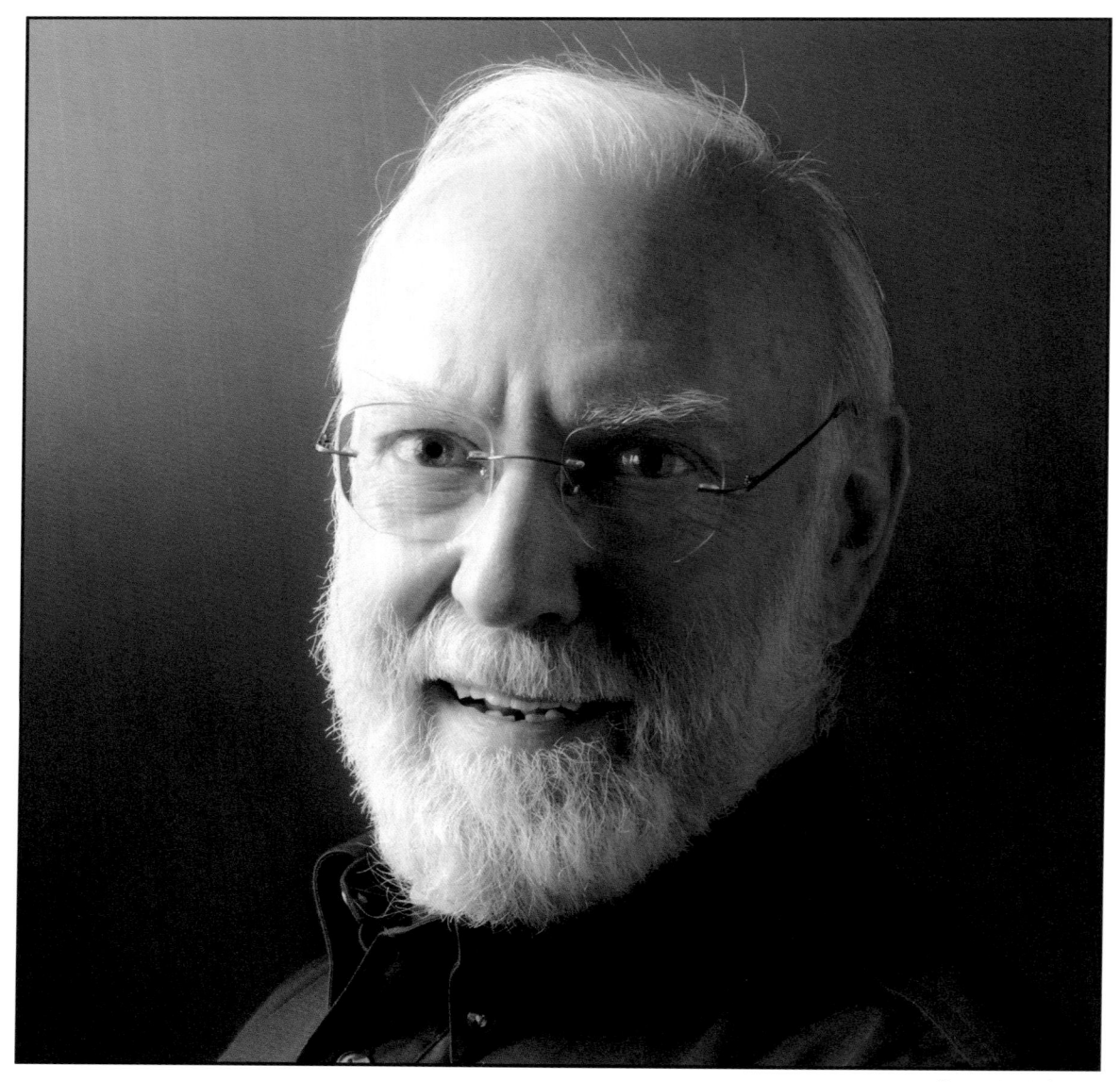

Dennis Adams

Start anywhere, from any direction,

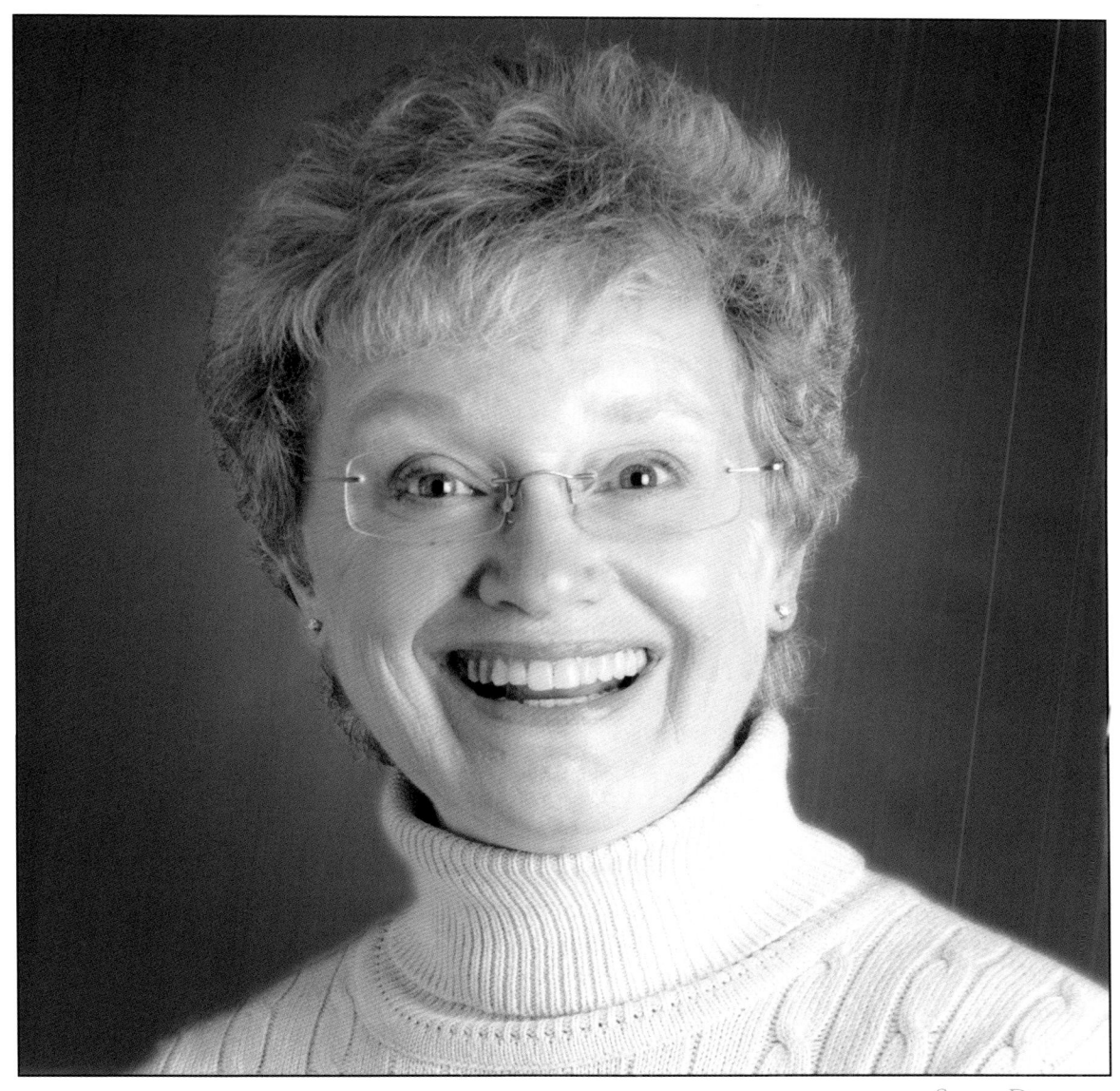

Susan Donovan

listen for laughter and breath.

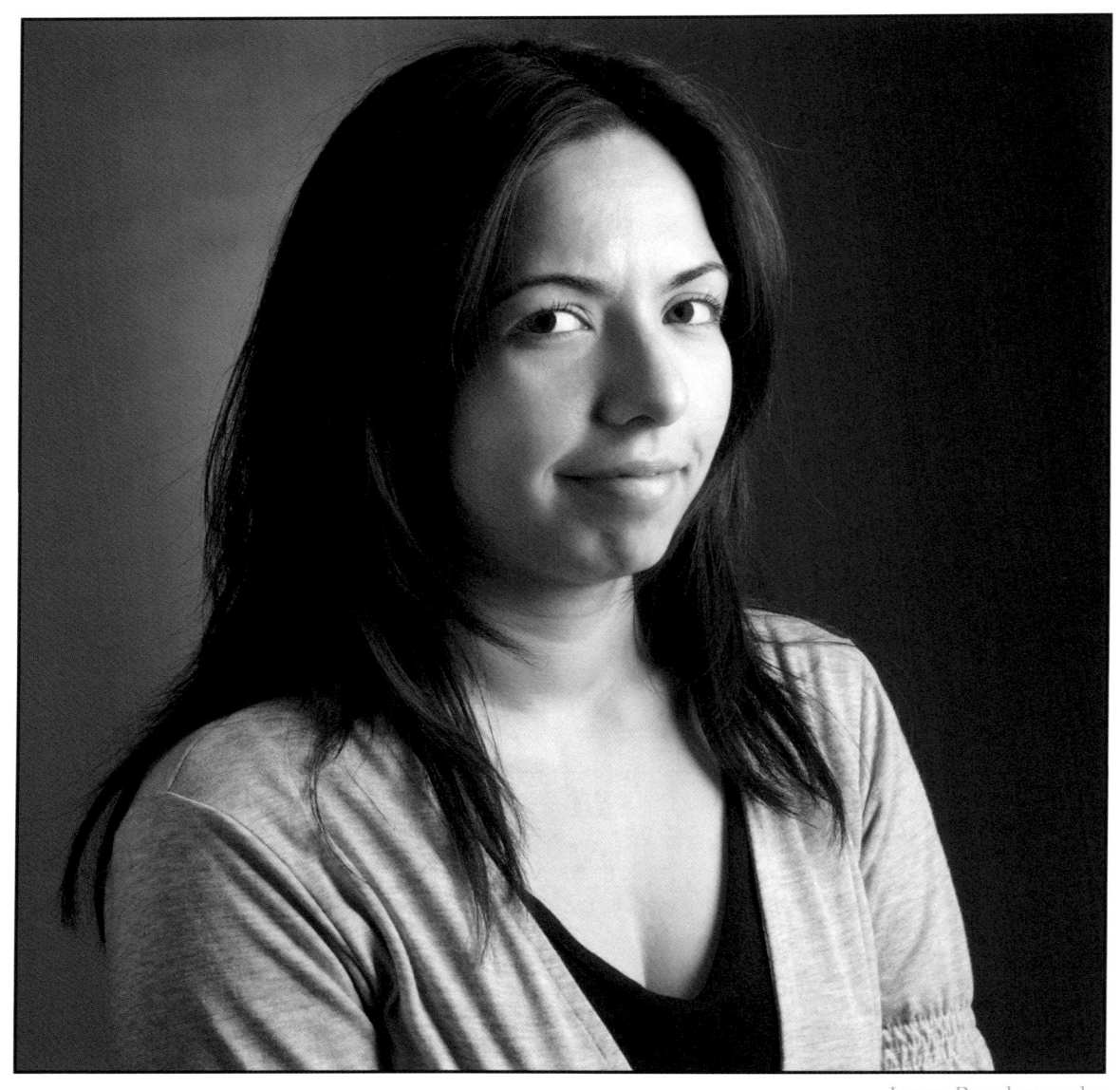

Watch as light lifts from the page:

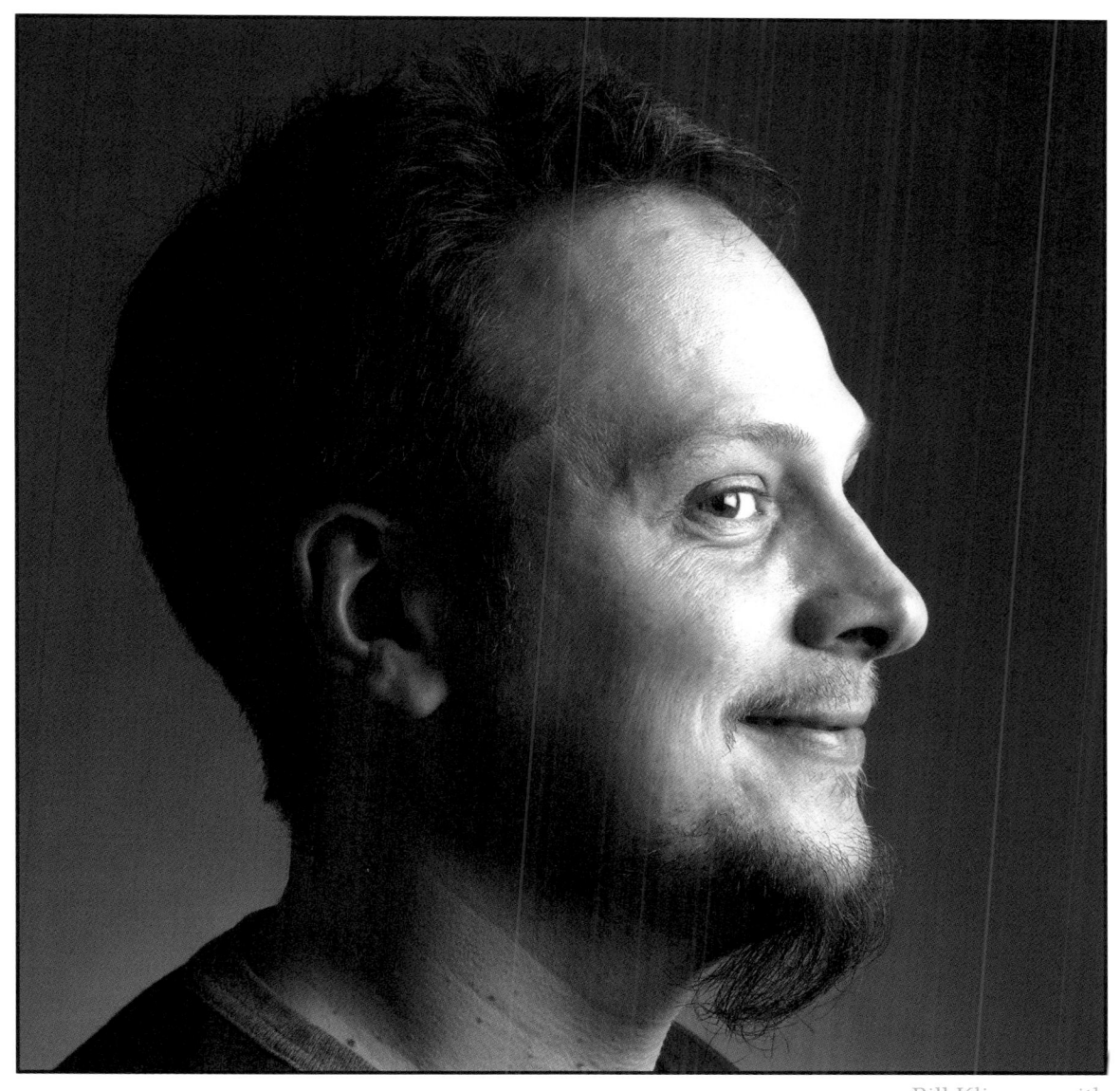

Bill Klingensmith

enter the eyes.

ENTER THE EYES

Anne C. Coon, Ph.D.

Confront the gaze
the camera seeks
pupil, lid, and lash.

Then enter the eyes
bright and black
lit from within
agleam.

The models beam
damp with uneasiness
carry props, as if from a treasure box:
clarinet, coffee cup, beads of stone.

Enter the eyes
of those who make music
bend light and words
send ideas soaring.

Teased out, unguarded,
they become
images of themselves
stories, melodies
pressed to the page.

Enter the eyes of women and men
stilled for a moment
their chatter suspended
joy and grief contained.

Consider the light on the brow
light springing from hands
hiding in a nest of beard
light palpable as paint
fragile as glass.

Enter the eyes
as professor becomes sitter
becomes subject
hair, whiskers, and spectacles
gloriously scrutinized;
wrinkles a landscape
shaped by the tide.

Watch for the hands
folded, ringed,
clenched to jaw, to elbow,
butterflied, pointing that-away
beyond the frame.

Enter the eyes
off center, winking, singular
twinned and twinged
cast skyward
dreaming of flight.

In an instant
hundreds of instants
the photographer hunts
fireflies in the dark
snap, catch, hold in a glass.

The pearls of a formulated phrase
the eyes have it
keep one on you
brown eyes, black eyes
green and blue eyes,
in the headlights, eyes.

How many tones from white
to black? How many pixels
between shadow and glow?
As many as the fractions
of the sitters themselves
countless, unedited,
caught by a click
faster than thought.

Come quietly, unburdened, curious.
Start anywhere, from any direction,
listen for laughter and breath.
Watch as light lifts from the page:
enter the eyes.

ARTIST'S STATEMENT
John Retallack

The wonderful thing about photography is . . . it is not about photography . . . it is about everything. The photography of people is about meeting people, learning their uniqueness and in general becoming familiar with them. In the process of this project, I have met colleagues from other colleges whom I have previously known only by reputation. Additionally, photographing colleagues from my own college I have become more aware of them. I've learned that this is an amazing community of artists and scientists. Collectively, they are an invaluable body of subjects for a photographer of people. Sadly, it has not been possible to capture an image of everyone; there are many I would have enjoyed photographing. Those who were available to me will have to suffice.

I have several reasons for working in black & white. First, the medium is an abstraction from reality. Next, it simplifies the difficulty of design given unpredictable wardrobe. Another is my long history of work in a wet darkroom. All images were captured in one of the SPAS studios using electronic flash and various digital cameras.

TECHNICAL DETAILS
Nitin Sampat

The continued development of digital presses by a variety of manufacturers provides publishers and printers many exciting opportunities for producing short-run, high-quality color "photo books." This book is the latest publication to emerge from an on-going print and publishing research project between RIT Cary Graphic Arts Press, faculty and students from RIT's College of Imaging Arts and Sciences, the print reproduction experts in RIT's Printing Applications Laboratory (PAL), and corporate partners HP (using its Indigo Press) and Mohawk Fine Papers (featuring its Super-fine line of premium papers).

The research team was presented with a challenging goal: to explore the capabilities of digital presses for reproducing black-and-white photographs, maintaining all of their highlights, sensuous midtones, and rich shadow areas. In the past, such images have been reproduced as duotones, tritones and even quadtones on an offset press. Achieving the same results on digital presses offers additional challenges in the workflow. Typically, digital presses use process color inks which makes it difficult to maintain neutrals in the image, and they deploy digital halftoning techniques that are limited by lower addressabilities. This fact makes it more difficult to simulate the continuous tone characteristics of the originals. The team decided to design two projects, each of which resulted in a separate publication, as follows.

Project One
The objective was to reproduce a collection of silver halide original black-and-white photographs using a custom inkset. The original images were captured using a

Betterlight camera and a workflow based on HP Artist, a proprietary software program developed at HP Labs, which used a generous sampling of spectral measurements taken from every print. This data was used to generate digital files that accurately captured the tone characteristics of the original photographs. These files were cropped and converted to grayscale (equal channel RGB). The exposure was adjusted and a minute amount of sharpening was added. A set of three custom gray inks and one black ink was selected (GGGK printing) and mixed at RIT's Printing Applications Laboratory. The HP Indigo 5500 Press was chosen for this project because of its superb image reproduction capabilities and the unique ability to equip it with custom-mixed inks.

The Mohawk Superfine i-Tone paper, in eggshell finish, was chosen for its exceptional reproduction characteristics. Its tone and texture also offered a close resemblance to the original prints. The press was calibrated with a custom test target and a mathematical printer model was designed and used to generate GGGK separations from the grayscale images. Using gray and black inks resulted in very smooth continuous tones with density levels as high as the matte paper permitted. The result was published in 2009 by Cary Graphic Arts Press under the title of *Mother Daughter*, by Elaine O'Neil.

Project Two

Here, the objective was to use a typical CMYK inkset to reproduce a collection of black-and-white photographs processed from images taken with a high-end digital camera. For the sake of consistency and comparison, the same press (Indigo) and paper (Superfine) were deployed. As noted above, the principal challenge in using a CMYK inkset is maintaining neutrality. Four strategies were considered:

1. Use maximum amount of black ink during GCR (Gray Component Replacement) for neutrality—at the expense of "continuous tone." This method would be least susceptible to day-to-day press variations. However, it also results in images that appear more "grainy" compared to the other approaches.

2. Use maximum CMY or CMY with very little black, while maintaining an acceptable density. This is generally the most expensive and unstable option, since digital presses often vary toward delivering an unacceptable pink cast in images. However, this approach would render the most "continuous tone" looking images. Our pragmatic solution to address the press variations would be to adjust curves on the images during the press run. The RIP has "curve adjustments" that can be used to help neutralize the images. However, this might have to made at periodic intervals throughout each day of printing. This is a unique approach and would produce

high quality images. The risk is the how often this would be need to be done in a given press run. Obviously, the higher the frequency of adjustments needed, the less practical this approach gets.

3. Use CMY selectively and generously (for example, in the "highlights" where added black would make them "grainy") while adding black as needed to increase "density." Typically this is done with black underneath the CMY but experiments would be conducted with different orderings of ink laydown, since the Indigo does allow for any order to be printed. This strategy renders images with a more "continuous tone," while not being as sensitive to press instability as the maximum CMY approach.

4. Characterize on-demand: Use different GCRs as described above, make a "ring around" set of test prints with differing amounts of CMYL and K. Pick one that is preferred by the Artist/Editor, profile the press for this choice, and convert all images to CMYK on the day of production printing. The press would be profiled each day for the duration of production and the strategy assumes press stability over a full working day. Any fluctuations or deviations from the "norm" would have to be watched for during the day's production run and fixed either with "curves" on the press or by reprofiling the images (a much more laborious and cumbersome) process. While this approach goes against the conventional wisdom of "early-binding" (having all images pre-processed and ready for printing), in BW printing, "press stability" is an absolute requirement and in digital printing such stability is hardly guaranteed.

The final choice was option 4 and resulted in the publication you now hold in your hands. Though there are many challenges in using a CMYK inkset for black-and-white printing, the implementation of a carefully planned workflow and rigorous color management offers publishers and printers with significant cost-saving benefits. As digital presses continue to evolve toward greater and greater stability, the characteristic color cast problems that have plagued black-and-white image reproduction will cease to be of concern.

ACKNOWLEDGMENTS

David Pankow, Director, RIT Cary Graphic Arts Press

With this publication, RIT Cary Graphic Arts Press continues its exploration of digital printing technologies. An earlier book, *Mother Daughter* (2009), by photographer and RIT Professor Elaine O'Neil, focused on the accurate reproduction of black-and-white photographs through the use of a custom inkset. The results were outstanding, and the book was acknowledged by photographers and graphic arts professionals as a milestone in digital reproduction technology. The Press was so grateful to the dedicated group of scientists, graphic arts specialists, and industry benefactors who made that publication possible that we asked them to consider a follow-up project!

This time, the subject material is a group of black-and-white studio photographs taken by photographer and RIT Professor John Retallack. My thanks to John and Anne for their moving collaboration.

The technical objective was to reproduce John's black-and-white images using the printer's standard inkset of cyan, magenta, yellow, and black (CMYK). In many ways, this was a more challenging task than using a custom inkset, and the reasons for this are fully explained in the Technical Details.

We again thank Nitin Sampat, a professor in RIT's School of Photographic Arts and Sciences for directing the research and experimentation into the subtleties of color reproduction on HP's superb Indigo digital press and the elusive search for the twin goals of neutrality and stability. RIT's formidable resources in digital press technology are largely centered in the Printing Applications Lab (PAL), directed by Bill Garno. Here, skilled technologists work with an array of digital presses and other resources to routinely resolve complex paper and ink issues for a worldwide clientele of manufacturers and users. PAL, along with its industry donors and supporters, continues to lead the way in perfecting the use of digital printing technology for high-quality color – and now black-and-white – image reproduction.

The Press is also grateful to Mohawk Fine Papers for donating its Superfine premium paper for this book. This extraordinarily versatile paper proved its worth in the offset environment. With its i-Tone configuration, Superfine is now taking a leadership position among preferred papers for the Indigo Press.

Finally, special thanks to Molly Cort, Managing Editor, for skillfully supervising the editorial matter and to Marnie Soom, Graphic Designer, for her beautiful cadences of photographs, poem, and text. All sponsors and contributors not otherwise acknowledged elsewhere in this publication are acknowledged in alphabetical order below.

Sponsors
For funding, facilities, and/or material support
Laura Field, Indigo Media Manager for the Americas, HP
Judy Finlay, Industrial Media Manger, HP, NA
Christopher Harrold, VP of Market Development, Emerging Print Technologies, Mohawk Fine Papers
Haim Levit, Category Business Manager, HP, NA

Contributors
For consultations, research, technical expertise, and/or production assistance
Dan Clark, Digital Printing Technologist
John Dettmer, Digital Systems Technologies, RIT PAL
Jeffrey DiCarlo, Principal Scientist, HP Labs
Gary Dispoto, Director, Print Production Automation Lab, HP Labs
Barbara Giordano, Operations Manager, RIT PAL
Wei Koh, Color Imaging Researcher, HP Labs
Franz Sigg, Senior Research Associate, School of Print Media

Name Index